KEN O'DONNELL is an Australian who h
1978. Ten years of life as an industrial chemis
led to a management consultancy in total quality management and process
re-engineering. He is the author of several books in Portuguese on diverse
subjects related to the development of human values: *The Last Frontier, Peace
Starts With You, Lessons For A Life of Fullness, The Soul of Business, The Roots
of Change* (published in Portuguese and Spanish) and *New Beginnings* (in
English and Japanese). Ken O'Donnell has conducted over a thousand talks,
courses and workshops in Australia, India, USA, Europe and Latin America
on stress management, positive consciousness, motivation, conflict
resolution, quality management and organisational development. He is the
co-ordinator of more than 30 branches of the Brahma Kumaris World
Spiritual University in South America.

Pathways

to Higher Consciousness

Ken O'Donnell

ETERNITY INK

Pathways
to Higher Consciousness

©1996 Brahma Kumaris Raja Yoga
Centres (Australia)

Published by
ETERNITY INK
77 Allen Street, Leichhardt NSW 2040
Australia www.bkmedia.com.au
bkmedia@ozemail.com.au
Printed January 1996
Reprinted October 1998
Reprinted January 2001
Reprinted November 2005

ISBN 0 646 26663 2

This book has been produced on behalf of
the Brahma Kumaris World Spiritual
University, a non-profit organisation, with
the aim to share information as a
community service for the spiritual growth
of individuals.
The Brahma Kumaris World Spiritual
University (BKWSU) exists to serve the
family of humanity: to assist individuals to
discover and experience their own
spirituality and personal growth, to
understand the significance and
consequences of individual action and
global interactions, and to reconnect and
strengthen their eternal relationship with
the Supreme Soul, the spiritual parent.

Contents

Introduction

OVER THE LAST century or even the last five years we have been witnesses to an unprecedented disintegration of many of our values, systems, customs and structures. Yet the crumbling down of so much that we hold dear has a positive side. It requires us to reconsider our approach to life. Our sometimes short-lived support systems have not brought the expected results. There is an unparalleled clamour for deeper understanding of the things of the spirit as if to say: enough is enough!

The search for new pathways has brought us back to our own selves and the hidden dimensions of a higher consciousness. Since the problems around us are the results of our deeds, it's a logical step to want to examine the seed of action – our consciousness itself. These other aspects of reality can be discovered by practical experiment within ourselves.

In spite of so much beauty and inspiration from the parables and examples of our traditions, world conditions appear to be worsening with time. On an individual level, our own practical lives rarely equate with our most honoured teachings.

An increasing number of people now find that meditation helps them to overcome the worries and stresses of modern life and obtain a state of calm that both refreshes the mind and relaxes the body. Though many see meditation as a way of achieving inner quiet, its wider significance is related to self empowerment. This is attained through an understanding and harnessing of the innate values that are latent in the self. The experiences that form the conceptual basis of this book have helped many thousands of people of all walks of life and religious backgrounds throughout the world to discover their deeper potential in coming to terms with change. If one word could describe this epoch, it would be 'change'. Change invites challenge – to look at the self and the situations around and to see how to balance these two distinct and yet interrelated worlds. Balance between the spiritual and the physical is the only valid response to the demands of life in this, the last decade of an incredible millennium.

It involves bringing reason and emotions into a state of equipoise, so that I can give rein to my truest feelings under the guidance of the steady hand of wisdom. I need to be aware of what is going on around me without being overwhelmed by it.

BACKGROUND TO THIS BOOK

I first made contact with the teachings of the Brahma Kumaris World Spiritual University in 1975 during a period of intense search. After journeying through many countries and having a first-hand experience of some of the world's major traditions, I was looking for something more than just answers. I was after fresh insights into living with myself and with the world around.

In spite of the wealth of different experiences in places like Thailand, India, Iran, Morocco and both Eastern and Western Europe, I was caught in my own personal maze from which I yearned to come out. I had succeeded in locking myself in the prison of my own head.

I was aware that mystics in Buddhism, Christianity, Hinduism, Islam and Judaism have for thousands of years drawn upon meditative techniques to deepen spiritual experience. My greatest difficulty was in finding people who were true to what they preached. I dearly wanted to set out towards the top of the mount of higher consciousness but realised I needed help.

I couldn't do it on my own.

Knocking on the door of the London branch of the Brahma Kumaris, I was greeted by a woman who radiated so much love and light that I was immediately intrigued and inspired to begin the study of this most ancient yet modern form of meditation called *Raja Yoga*. I was advised to experiment with the ideas. I was encouraged to put the ideas I understood and accepted into practice as much as possible. Having had my fill of words and ideas, I was unprepared simply to study yet another body of knowledge and remain on the same theoretical level to which I had been accustomed. I was an expert at impressing friends by what I knew of things of the spirit but my real life was in a state of confusion. The purely practical approach I had now discovered, appealed to me profoundly. I've been studying and practising Raja Yoga meditation ever since.

ABOUT THE SPIRITUAL UNIVERSITY

The international headquarters of the Brahma Kumaris World Spiritual University is nestled between the hills in the town of Mount Abu in the Aravali Range in northwestern India. Its popular name is *Madhuban* which means *Forest of Honey*. The sweetness, divine detachment and wisdom that permeate the place attract students and visitors from all over the world.

At its more than 3,500 branches in over 60 countries the activities are free of charge. Cost is not a barrier for those wishing to do the many different courses offered. The centres are maintained by voluntary contributions from those who are taking benefit from the studies.

The university operates both on the individual and community levels, making a valuable contribution through courses and lectures concerning life skills, development of inner potential and positive thinking. For the individual, the central theme is the study and practice of Raja Yoga meditation. This becomes a method for activating our inner spiritual qualities so that self-change can become a real experience.

For regular students the university divides studies into four main areas: knowledge of the inner and outer aspects of human life; the practice of meditation; the conscious assimilation of quality behavioural characteristics; serving the community at large.

For the community, many projects are carried out. They are aimed at raising the awareness of personal responsibility in helping solve such wide-ranging social problems as lack of adequate education and health, environmental imbalance, family disharmony, drug abuse and human rights abuses.

In recognition for its work in communities around the world the university became affiliated to the United Nations in 1980 as a Non-Governmental Organisation. Consultative status on the Roster of the UN Economic and Social Council followed in 1983, and with UNICEF in 1987. In that year, the university received the title of Peace Messenger Organisation from the U.N. for its work in peace education worldwide. It has co-ordinated several international projects including 'Million Minutes of Peace' and 'Global Co-operation for a Better World'.

ABOUT THIS BOOK

This book is based on the teachings that came through the founder of the university, Prajapita Brahma, and classes of its senior teachers over many years. These are worked in with my own personal experiences with Raja Yoga since 1975. The chapters reflect the sequence of the introductory course on Raja Yoga meditation that is the foundation for those who wish to become regular students.

No matter what your experience of meditation has been, if you study Raja Yoga with sincerity and an open mind, the benefits will be immediate. Raja Yoga meditation doesn't demand belief but invites experiment. If the student impartially measures the ideas contained herein against his/her own thinking, then what is felt to be useful can be applied directly to practical life. This can give strength and clarity to tackle deeper concepts. The objective is not to convert anyone but to enrich lives.

ABOUT RAJA YOGA MEDITATION

Raja Yoga is the art of living in balance — of being happy and peaceful, of knowing and loving the self and others on a deeper, more spiritual level. It's an essentially spiritual practice that has its roots in antiquity and yet its validity is confirmed in the present day-to-day personal whirlwinds of many.

Just as there are forms of *yoga* that seek to improve the muscular tone and mobility of the physical body, Raja Yoga deals with the inner organisation, transformation and empowerment of my more subtle faculties of thinking, deciding and personality traits.

Its usefulness is experienced especially in the ease with which it helps me cope with adverse situations. The development of strengths and the overcoming of weaknesses are constant proofs that I can truly be a much better and more effective human being than I previously imagined.

I have to deal with many things in life for which my formal education perhaps hasn't prepared me. In a peaceful atmosphere I may be happy and have enough resolve to carry on, but when the going is rough, perhaps there is not sufficient power to face, adapt and change. Unless I have access to my inner resources, then understanding alone will not help me.

The word *yoga* comes from the Sanskrit root *yug* which means link or bond. In that sense, if I remember something or someone, it can be said that I am having *yoga* with that object or person. The word *raja* means *sovereign* or *king*. Of all the possible things I can remember or think about, the most elevated or sovereign would definitely be God. Thus, Raja Yoga refers to the mental link between the human soul and the Supreme Being or God, which generates sovereignty or mastery over the physical senses and over our thoughts, words and actions.

In other words, Raja Yoga meditation is a two-step process:

1. Joining the scattered forces of my thoughts and fixing them on my true self.
2. Having stabilised them, I can then make the connection with the Supreme Being and begin to absorb the unlimited spiritual energy emanating from that One.

It's a very personal effort and, as it happens on the level of the inner self, it can be practised by people of any religious persuasion or even those without any. After all, before I am a Christian, Buddhist, Jew or Muslim, I am simply a being. Raja Yoga meditation operates on the level of the being and its relationship with God.

One of the possible roots of the word *meditate* is the Latin *medire* which means *to heal*. The whole process of Raja Yoga meditation is an inner healing which involves acquiring the power to let go of whatever is negative in the make-up of the self.

It also means being able to know and dialogue with the self. With deeper self-appreciation, I get the courage to eliminate weaknesses without guilt or regret. In silence I am able to speak with the inner self and develop a link with the Supreme Being in order to heal myself. There are no magic formulae that can bring about mental calm. It's a step-by-step process with three basic requirements: understanding of spiritual knowledge, practice of that understanding through meditation and patience in waiting for the results to become apparent.

Good luck on your journey!

Ken O'Donnell

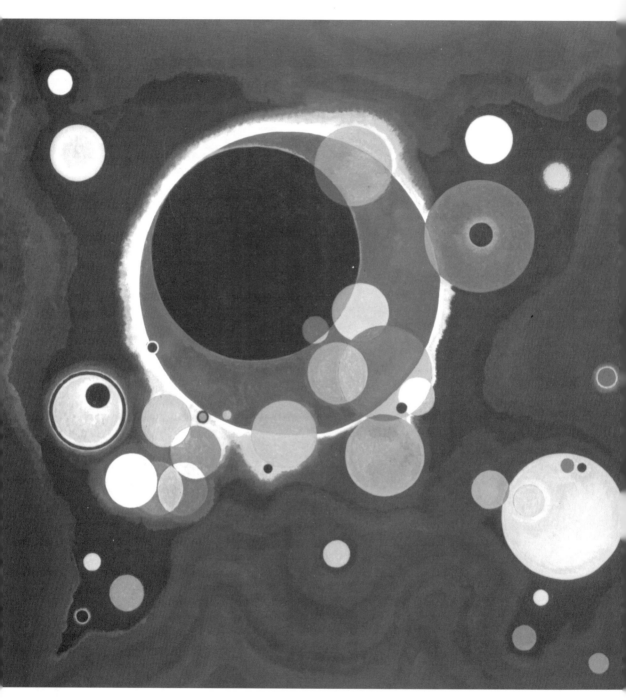

*For Vasily Kandinsky the circle represents a development in cosmic evolution parallel
to that of spirit taking the form of matter.
(Vasily Kandinsky "Several Circles" Guggenheim Museum)*

Chapter 1

Soul and Matter

Stepping into the dimension of the spirit is a very subtle process, mainly because the mind is locked into a vision of reality that excludes eternity. Matter, the senses and things of immediate interest so dominate my thoughts that the very nature of existence becomes distorted. I see the world not as it is but as I am.

My life revolves within narrow limits, distinctions and desires as I play the game of labelling myself and others on the basis of purely physical characteristics. I divide the world according to sex, race, creed, nation, age and social status and put everyone into his or her little box.

Because of such division there is conflict in and around me as I seek to defend the territory thus established – whether it be a role, a job, a position in society, the family name or a nation. 'May no one encroach upon my territory' is an unspoken sign planted in my heart.

Taking off the glasses of what can be termed body-consciousness, through which I see and judge the world around, calls for some effort. To experience the soul or self in its true light requires a detailed understanding of the terms and processes used. But the very act of taking such a step opens up a whole new perspective of seeing and reacting to the world around me.

With insight into the true nature of things, the very same life that I am leading in terms of work, family and leisure, becomes the springboard for my own transformation.

Letting go of the consciousness of the limits of this physical body and experiencing the inner self or soul is the essence of Raja Yoga.

Disorder and tension on an individual, and consequently, social level are the result of ignorance of the self and the world around. The mind stays without rest, running, jumping and churning aimlessly, lashed by waves of feelings and emotions. Like a spider caught in its own web, I become entangled in nets which are the consequences of my own ignorance of the fundamentals of life.

In this chapter I begin a journey that will take me through deeper and deeper levels of understanding and experience which create freedom from these nets. This chapter deals with:

✪ The difference between soul and matter: the metaphysical and the physical.
✪ The difference between *I* and *my*.
✪ The position, form and attributes of the soul.
✪ The first steps in meditation.
✪ The distinction between the soul and matter.

In life many happenings cannot be explained solely in material terms. At certain points of crisis or inspiration, there are deep emotional and spiritual experiences which separate me from the world around. I retreat at such times, into myself, into religious or philosophical books, into rituals or symbols, in order to understand them. I am subject to a perpetual commentary on life around me from my own thoughts, feelings and deductions.

These faculties of thinking and forming ideas, desiring and deciding (and all the different aspects which constitute my individual personality) are non-physical, and yet real. Indeed, anything perceptible to me comes from two sources: what is detected by the physical senses and what arises from impressions recorded on these subtle faculties. The things that I can see, taste, hear, smell and feel, as well as the body itself, are formed of matter. But the subtle faculties of mind, intellect and personality are manifestations of what is called *consciousness*.

Consciousness is another word for soul or spirit. The soul is a subtle entity that cannot be measured by any physical process or instrumentation. The non-material part of each one of us exists, and is in fact the true self or what we simply call *I*. This *I*, or soul, is perceptible only at the level of mind and intellect.

ATOM AND ATMA

Throughout history scientists have built up knowledge of the laws of the physical universe on the foundation of atomic theory. The atom is seen to be a point-source of energy, and different energy levels and vibrations between neighbouring atoms give the appearance of form, colour and heat. Atomic theory appeared originally in Greece and in India.

The English word *atom* came from the Latin *atomus* which means *the twinkling of an eye* and the Greek *atomos* meaning *indivisible*. The Greek word probably derives from the Hindi *atma* which means *self* or *soul* and refers to the conscious energy of the human as being an indivisible and indestructible point of non-physical light.

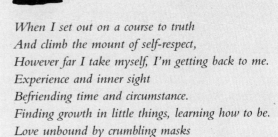

When I set out on a course to truth
And climb the mount of self-respect,
However far I take myself, I'm getting back to me.
Experience and inner sight
Befriending time and circumstance.
Finding growth in little things, learning how to be.
Love unbound by crumbling masks
Opens doors within the self.
Nothing comes to break the link.
It brings me back to me.

It has been established that the entire material world I see around me as a variety of forms and colours, light and heat, is formed of these point-sources of physical energy. The most beautiful scene in nature is merely a pattern of energy waves and vibrations.

The sense organs select the vibrations and relay a message to the mind where all images are formed. The eyes see some of these patterns as light forms and colours, the nose receives odours, tastes and sensations are detected and transmitted to the mind.

The human body is also a complex pattern of physical energies. Atoms come together to form the organic structures and inorganic minerals which perform the body's chemical interactions, thus forming the basis of the hormonal and nervous control of the body.

What I see as old or young, ugly or beautiful, male or female, is also the effect of these differing levels of physical energies. However marvellous a machine the body may be, it is the presence of the soul which makes it function.

One of the basic differences between souls and atoms is that while souls can exercise choice of their movements, where to go and when to go somewhere, atoms cannot obviously exercise such choice. In a way you could say that a soul is a point-source of spiritual energy that has awareness of its own existence. Atoms do not.

DEFINITIONS

The word *atma* has three specific meanings — I, the living being and the dweller. Within this one word we get an insight into different aspects of the self: I, the living being, am the dweller within this physical body.

The answer to the question, Who am I? becomes clear. I am the soul, the living and intelligent inner being. I inhabit and give life to the body. The body is the means through which I, the soul, express myself and experience the world around me. Instead of answering the question as to my identity by giving the name of the body, the job designation, nationality or gender, the real inner self can simply say: I am the soul; I have a body. The basic differences are shown in the table on the following page.

DIFFERENCE BETWEEN
THE SOUL & THE BODY

Immortal	Mortal
Eternal, no beginning or end	Is born and dies
Metaphysical	Physical
Unlimited	Limited
Pure conscious energy	Made up of matter

THE LIVING AND THE DEAD The table below shows simple distinctions but the implications are far-reaching. The differences are clearest when comparing a dead corpse with a living body.

When the soul leaves the body, it's not just the body that dies but it's as if all the connections with the world of that individual are simply switched off. Not only the relationships but all specific plans, projects and desires suddenly have no further means through which they can be expressed or cultivated. The faculties of thinking, deciding and the personality traits connected with the life that is being left behind, stop and go into a momentary state of latency to emerge again in a new body, a new life. All the material things that belonged to that particular individual are passed on to others.

It's interesting to note that even when the body is sick it can only be treated when the soul is still present. If we take out the soul, no one remains to look after the body.

On the other hand, the body is a truly marvellous vehicle for the soul to express itself through. No manufactured machine could hope to compete. For example, it is calculated that in just one day, the brain is able to complete a hundred times more connections than the entire telecommunications system of the planet. Or compare the human eye with any manufactured camera or the heart with any manufactured pump. The body's importance cannot be played down.

THE SOUL IS NEITHER MALE NOR FEMALE

As an energy, the soul has within itself qualities that are both masculine and feminine. Though the soul is certainly affected by the gender of its body in the form of conditioning and social influences, those aspects are relatively superficial. The real self has no gender.

The ancient Egyptians were strongly aware of this deep truth, as shown in the following excerpt of a conversation in the Egyptian Book of the Dead between Isis and her son Horus:

Horus: How are souls born, male or female?

Isis: Souls, my son Horus, are all equal in nature... There are none among them either men or women; this distinction only exists between bodies, and not between incorporeal beings...

SYNONYMS FOR SOUL

The following words are essentially synonyms for the word *soul:*

- ✪ Spirit
- ✪ Being
- ✪ Consciousness
- ✪ Inner self
- ✪ Anima/animus
- ✪ Life energy
- ✪ Essence
- ✪ I

DIFFERENCE BETWEEN 'I' AND 'MY'

The two most common words in most languages are probably *I* and *my*. Our personal worlds almost revolve exclusively around them. I have to understand their deeper implications if I want to redesign my limits.

I normally use the word *my* to refer to all the things that are not me – *my* hand, *my* face, *my* leg or even *my* brain, *my* mind, *my* personality and so on. The next time I catch myself saying *my* soul, I could perhaps remember that I can't really say *my* soul if I am the soul.

The difference between *I* and *my* is the as that same between the soul and the body. The example of a knife illustrates this. I can use it to cut a tomato or to stab someone. The knife neither decides nor experiences, but can be washed easily under the tap. Now look at the fingers which held the knife. They neither decide nor experience the actions. They too can be washed under the tap. It's easy to realise that the knife is an instrument, but it is more difficult to realise that the fingers are instruments too, and not only the fingers but also the arms.

PERSONAL EXPERIENCE

As I sat down, I tried to think of myself as a spiritual being, a point-source of conscient energy centred in the forehead. After some minutes I became aware that my attention was leaving the various limbs and organs of the body. It was as if there was a rush of energy rising slowly like mercury in a thermometer, towards the area in the centre between the eyebrows. Then very suddenly I had the feeling that I was totally bodiless, without any weight or heaviness. There was a deep feeling of detachment from the physical surroundings. Even though I was acutely aware of the things around, I was seeing them completely in the observer state; I was just a tiny point of consciousness, surrounded by a lot of movement, forms, colours and sounds of which I was not part.

The legs are instruments for walking, the eyes for seeing, the ears for hearing, the mouth for speaking, breathing and tasting, the heart for pumping food and oxygen around the body, and so on. Even the brain is like a computer used to express all thought, word and action programmes through the body and to experience the results. If every physical part of the body is an instrument, who or what is it that is using it?

Very simply it is I, the self, the soul. The soul uses the word *I* for itself and the word *my* when referring to the body; *my* hand, *my* mouth, *my* brain. *I* am different from *my* body.

Through the consciousness of *my*, I have spread myself far and wide — not only with regard to the body and inner faculties but in relation to possessions and relationships — *my* house, *my* car, *my* son and so on. With time, all of these things which I try to hold to myself, slip through my fingers. I realise their temporary nature and for want of available alternatives I try to clutch onto them even more and thus develop attachments and dependencies. While this identification persists, my innate qualities, (i.e. what's really mine) are out of reach. When I assume my true identity as a spiritual being, then I also immediately have access to the love, peace, happiness and power that are part of me.

If I make a list of all the factors which create limits for me, it would probably include things like age, sex, health, family, profession, defects and weaknesses. By claiming ownership of all these through the word *my*, I set the boundaries within which I try to operate my life. Having set up my own fences, whenever sorrow appears, one or the other of these becomes the unwitting scapegoat.

Instead of pointing the finger of blame or complaining, I can adopt a more positive approach. I can be more realistic and accept them not as limiting factors but as instruments through which I can improve my experience of life. This same list can be the springboard for my transformation and freedom.

I can make full use of the adult state or the energy of youth as the case may be. I can take advantage of the positive characteristics of my gender whilst appreciating those of the other. My family and professional life can be experienced on another more elevated level. I can observe in my weaknesses and defects how much I have to learn about myself. The problem is not in the list of factors but in the consciousness I have towards them. It is a question of two words — *I* and *my*.

SOUL – POSITION, FORM AND ATTRIBUTES

The dualities of matter/antimatter, sentient/insentient, physical/spiritual can be understood easily with the awareness of the mechanism by which human consciousness operates through the body. The soul has three basic functions to perform: to give and maintain life, to express and experience its own unique life and to receive the rewards or fruits of past actions performed in previous existences.[1]

1 See Chapter 4 on Karma.

POSITION

When I look in a mirror I don't see my reflection but that of my body. The soul is actually looking through the windows of the eyes from some point inside the head. The sentient functions are controlled and monitored through the nervous and hormonal systems from a particular point in the area of the brain housing the thalamus, hypothalamus, pituitary and pineal glands. This region is known as the seat of the soul or the third eye. The connection between the physical and the non-physical is by the medium of thought energy. When viewed from the front, this region appears to be between and slightly above the line of the eyebrows.

Many religions, philosophies and esoteric studies place great importance on the third eye or eye of the mind. The Hindus use a *tilak,* a dot in red or sandalwood paste in the middle of the forehead. Christians also make the sign of the cross with their thumb in this region. The Muslims also touch that spot in their traditional salute. When anyone of any culture makes a foolish mistake, the person instinctively brings his hand to that spot. After all, it's not the body that makes the mistake but the thinking being that is operating the body from that particular point. As the brain is the control centre for all of the various processes of the body – metabolism, the nervous, endocrine, immunological, and lymphatic systems – it makes sense that the inner person be located somewhere in the brain.

Just as the driver in a car sits behind the wheel with the steering wheel in his hands, the soul sits in a specific

When I look in a mirror, I don't see my reflection but that of my body.
The soul looks through the windows of the eyes.

point in the centre of the brain near the pineal body. This is important to know for meditation purposes because it is the place to which attention is first directed in the effort to concentrate the thoughts: I am the soul, a tiny point of conscious light energy centred in the spot between the brows.

Whenever I say: I feel something within me, pointing to the heart, obviously it's not something within the chest. The physical heart is just an incredibly sophisticated pump for blood. It can even be transplanted! Within the real me, the living and thinking being, there is a centre of emotions, moods and feelings.

The sensations that I very obviously feel around the body are due to the total interconnectedness that exists between the soul and the matter that it is inhabiting. For example, when I am afraid of, say, a dog attacking me, the whole system is activated. From the control centre in the middle of the brain,

PERSONAL EXPERIENCE

In the Fourth Brazilian Congress on Quality and Productivity in 1994 I had been given a time-slot at 6 pm in the afternoon on the third day. At 5:30 I walked into the auditorium and found that more than a third of the 800 participants were dozing after having been listening for three solid days. In front of the convention centre there were the municipal markets where I had the inspiration to go and buy a coconut.

With my purchase I walked on stage, picked up the microphone after the introductions and addressed the audience. "If you were kids from Northern Russia," I asked them, "what would you think of this coconut? Having never seen one in your lives, you would probably not believe me if I told you that it had very delicious white flesh and liquid inside. Seeing its hairiness you probably would scoff at such a suggestion. In order to show you I'd have to break it open."

That's exactly what I did on the edge of the stage. Certainly the audience became alert as they waited for the explanation.

As an individual I am like the coconut. The hard and hairy shell of the ego prevents me from realising that within me there is a soft core of inner qualities that are the real sources of sustenance for myself and my relationships. The shell cannot sustain anyone.

the soul sends messages out all around the body. Adrenalin is liberated to give extra strength to the muscles. The heart starts to pump faster, the breathing becomes shallower and the palms begin to sweat. While it may seem that all the different organs have autonomous sensing and feeling systems, the whole operation is so split-second fast that the coordination of sensations and responses by the soul from its own special cockpit in the centre of the brain passes unnoticed. In this way, if I feel something in my heart for or from something or someone, it's really being processed by me, the thinking being, and then reflected in my heart.

FORM

All of the characteristics present in the soul are subtle or non-dimensional in nature – thoughts, feelings, emotions, decision-making power, personality traits and so on. If they are all without size, then it is reasonable to conclude that the conscious energy from which they emerge is also sizeless. For this simple reason it is eternal. Something which has no physical size cannot be destroyed.

As a soul I am neither diffused throughout the whole body nor am I an invisible or ethereal duplicate of the physical body. Even though this subtle form exists, it is the effect of the soul being in the physical form and not the soul itself. Just as the sun is in one place and yet its light radiates throughout the solar system, the soul is in one place and its energy permeates the whole body.

To express something that exists but has no physical dimensions we can use the word *point*. The soul therefore, is an infinitesimal point of conscient light. For the sake of having an image to fix our minds on we can say it's star like in appearance. In deep meditation I can perceive the soul as an infinitesimal point of non-physical light surrounded by an oval-shaped aura.

INNATE QUALITIES OF THE SOUL

Everything I see has what can be called its acquired value and its innate or inherent value. The acquired value is that which it has picked up directly by association throughout its existence. The innate value is what it always is irrespective of its appearances. For example, the acquired value of gold changes with the fluctuations of the market-place. Its real or innate value is that it's one of the most beautiful of minerals. It is extremely ductile and malleable and so on.

If I were asked about the main qualities present in a harmonious relationship with someone, I could immediately reply: love, patience, tolerance, understanding, empathy and so on. How do I know this? Is it purely from experience? Can I remember having really experienced any of these qualities in any relationship fully and constantly? Probably not. In that case, where does this urge for rightness come from if not from an innate sense of what is true and good?

How can I judge or perceive the level of peace, love or happiness in a situation except by a projection of these same qualities that are within me? It's as if they join together as a subtle ruler for measuring what goes on around me so that necessary internal adjustments can be made according to the situation. If it is good or bad, peaceful or confused, my own innate qualities at least advise me as to what is going on.

The problem is that they are in a latent state and do not translate very easily into action. Though these qualities are the basis of my ideals, when I am in a weakened state I am unable to bring them into practice at will,

Each human is a unique combination of attributes. We are inspired to seek and to dream by the innate perfection awaiting us when these attributes are again emerged and balanced.

according to the demands of the moment. They need to be empowered.

One of the most immediate benefits of the practice of meditation then, is to improve the functioning of this inner ruler. My innate qualities are just waiting for a chance to manifest themselves. Like a light bulb without current, the possibility of lighting up my qualities exists, but they need to be connected to a source of power. This is exactly what meditation brings.

Innate attributes are properties that are immutable. It's impossible to take the blue out of the sky or sweetness out of honey. Blueness and sweetness are part of the unchanging make-up of sky and honey.

In the same way, in spite of whatever I have become as a human individual, my deep innate attributes are still the same ones that have always existed in me. It's my inner core of qualities that in fact inspires me to seek the ideal in whatever I do. If someone were to ask me a list of qualities that are important in a relationship between two people, things like respect, honesty, sincerity, openness and so on would automatically spring to mind. Even if I have never experienced them in living memory, I still seek them. The impulse to seek and to dream comes from my own store of innate attributes that is just waiting to be found and brought into practical activity.

The innate qualities of the soul are those that are the most fundamental. They are so basic that they themselves are the basis of all virtues and powers.

✪ Peace   ✪ Truth   ✪ Happiness   ✪ Love
✪ Purity   ✪ Power   ✪ Balance

They are like primary colours and virtues are secondary. Just as green is made of blue and yellow, virtues such as patience, tolerance, courage, sweetness and so on are compounds of these basic qualities. Some examples:

Patience — peace, love and power

Courage — power and truth

Discernment — truth, peace and balance

The objective of Raja Yoga meditation is to empower my own innate attributes so that my behaviour can be naturally virtuous.

THE INNER FACULTIES OF THE SOUL

The body consists of many organs and limbs to move around and exist in the physical world. So too, the soul has the subtle faculties of thinking power (mind), reasoning power (intellect) and its own unique personality to negotiate the inner world of thoughts, feelings, decisions and habits.

> The essential functions of the mind are:
> THOUGHT
> IMAGINATION
> CREATION OF IDEAS
> SENSATION
> DESIRE
> FEELING
> EMOTION

The understanding of how they work and integrate helps me immensely in putting my personal world in order. To fix a machine it's good to know how it works. In the same way, if I comprehend the workings of my internal process of thinking, deciding and becoming, I can start to repair myself. The soul expresses itself through the mind (thoughts, desires, feelings), the intellect (willpower – which discerns and judges) and the *sanskars* [2] (personality traits, habits and so on). What is the importance of each faculty?

MIND

If I want to change my life, I need to change my actions, for which I have to alter my thinking. To do that I need to know just how and why thoughts arise.

The soul uses the mind as a screen or field on which it projects thoughts, sensations, images and ideas. According to the impact that they cause, an experience, feeling or emotion is created. For example, if I think "banana", immediately the familiar curved and yellow image of a banana appears on the mental screen together with, perhaps, the sensation of its taste or texture. If I remember something abstract like my work colleague's defect of irresponsibility, it brings with it a feeling of negativity, perhaps related to something I

---

2 *We have decided to retain the word sanskars in its original Hindi as it is difficult to translate well. It means the subconscious and unconscious impressions that form the basis of the personality.*

haven't quite worked out in myself.

Basically, what happens is that the mind has the amazing capacity to take on the form of whatever it is thinking about at any one moment and extract a feeling of the quality that comes with the form. Nothing could be a greater incentive towards positive thinking than this simple fact. If I want to feel good, I have to have the types of thoughts that bring the quality of goodness.

The mind is unfortunately subject to the whims and inconsistencies of the intellect. Just as the tides are pulled by the force of gravity to whatever the side of the world the moon happens to be on, the tides of the mind are its moods. Wherever the intellect roams, the mind automatically follows producing all of its essential functions.

INTELLECT

As the ruler of the inner state, the intellect is the principal faculty of the self. While a powerful and benign ruler is of immense benefit to any country, a weak and confused leader is manipulated and over-ruled by clever subjects. The feeble and befuddled intellect subjugates itself to two worlds: the external world of the senses and their objects, and the internal world of thoughts, feelings and personality traits.

If I want peace, then I need an intellect that can create and decide on the types of

> The key functions of the intellect are:
>
> DECISION–MAKING
>
> DISCERNMENT OR DISCRIMINATION POWER
>
> REASONING POWER
>
> THE ABILITY TO REMEMBER, ASSOCIATE AND IDENTIFY
>
> WILL–POWER
>
> THE ABILITY TO UNDERSTAND, KNOW AND RECOGNISE
>
> JUDGEMENT

thought patterns and actions that lead to peace. In this way, the peace-provoking *sanskars* can be reinforced and brought to the surface so that they are the ones that come into the mind. Thus the intellect plays its role of door-keeper. It allows or refuses entry into the process according to its own set of rules and perceptions. Through meditation the accuracy of this role is heightened so that positive qualities are permitted entry and continuity while negative ones are weakened and transformed.

The intellect can really be strengthened for this vital purpose through meditation and vigilance. Understanding of what is necessary is not enough. I can know, for example, that to become irritated is detrimental to my life. Even so, when I am faced by the person who has been a traditional trigger for my irritation and once again he is doing exactly that action which I find so annoying, then all theory is of no use. At that moment I need power not to get irritated. Meditation will give me that power.

The strength or weakness of an individual is connected with the intellect. It's important to note that an individual can have an intellect that functions

> **All of the following are** *sanskars:*
> HABITS
> TENDENCIES
> PERSONALITY TRAITS
> MEMORIES
> VALUES
> BELIEFS
> LEARNING
> TALENTS
> INSTINCT

perfectly well without necessarily being an intellectual.

SANSKARS

The soul is the seed which contains within itself not only the faculties of thinking and deciding but has a specific configuration. Just as each chemical element's structure and reactability is based on its electron/proton arrangement, the soul's config-uration is based on what are known as *sanskars*. This word is very inadequately translated as *personality traits*. A more accurate description would be the imprints that are the basis of the personality. It largely resembles what is called in the West 'sub-conscious mind', though it also includes the unconscious as well.

When I am in bed at night just before going off to sleep, images of all shapes, forms and colour pour onto the screen of the mind one after the other. Of course, it's not only when I am dreaming that the *sanskars* come into play.

The raw material for all thoughts, ideas, feelings and emotions also arise from the *sanskars*. In the analogy of images projected on a screen the *sanskars* would be the archives of all previously recorded experiences.

Every single action that I perform leaves its mark in the soul itself as a *sanskar*. The tendency of the *sanskars* to self-organise means that they group themselves according to quality and function.

The above characteristics are the basis of our individual uniqueness. The quality of a person when described by such adjectives as good, evil, happy-natured, boring, arrogant, altruistic and so on, is basically related to his or her *sanskars*.

HOW THESE THREE FACULTIES WORK TOGETHER

The three aspects of the self work together in a precise and integrated manner. Each faculty affects both the others. Functioning jointly they produce what can be termed the state of consciousness [3].

Looking at the flow in a clockwise direction we can see how from the *sanskars* a thought arises in the mind which is processed by the intellect. The intellect decides whether to carry it into action or not through the body. If the decision is to act, the experience of the action is recorded in the soul as a *sanskar*.

In this way old *sanskars* (those that are already there) are modified, strengthened or weakened according to the actions performed. In the case of a thought not being carried through into action, it is simply tossed back into the pool of sanskars for future consideration if necessary.

---

3 Further details in Chapter 2.

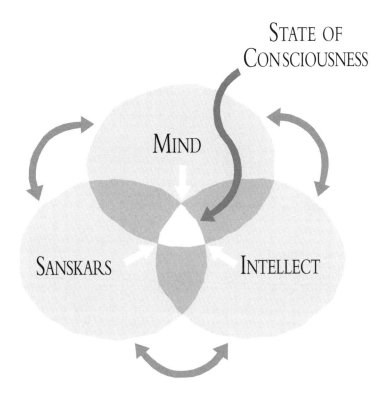

CONCLUSIONS FROM UNDERSTANDING THE PROCESS OF THE SELF

The main points that I can take from this are:

✪ The intellect has a crucial role in guiding and transforming the self.

✪ I cannot escape the effects of whatever I do.

✪ I have within me both the sources of any suffering I may go through as well as the solutions to it.

✪ The positive qualities which are in me as *sanskars* can only be brought to the surface of the conscious mind through intervention by the intellect.

From the diagram above I can understand that thought is the seed of action and experience. When there is the desire for pure experience, coupled with the realisation of the importance of the quality of thought, then naturally there is the desire to select those seeds which will bear the desired fruit. If I desire peace, knowledge, contentment, love, power, joy and so on, there will be the aim to control or eradicate those thoughts and sanskars which are the seeds of disharmony and peacelessness. The mechanism by which the soul can select its desired thoughts and emotions is the intellect.

In the formation of my *sanskars* there are obviously some experiences that have been positive and beneficial for me, while others have been non-beneficial or harmful. I can ask myself the following questions:

✪ Has a particular thought come from a *sanskar* of disharmony or peacelessness?

✪ Will this thought bring me or others further peacelessness?

✪ Will it create harmony and respect in others?

✪ How can I strengthen the *sanskars* of bringing benefit?

INTELLECT - WILLPOWER

The expression *willpower* is often used to refer to my ability to put into practice the ideals I know to be for my wellbeing and to resist activity which is harmful. This is directly related to the strength of the intellect. When we speak of weakness or strength in the soul, we are referring to the intellect. In the case of the weak soul, it is almost as if the intellect plays no part in determining which thoughts arise in the mind, but they come as if driven by the *sanskars* (mainly in the form of habits) or are triggered by the atmosphere or by the moods of others. On the contrary, a powerful soul enjoys the experience of its own choice regardless of external stimuli.

Raja Yoga develops the intellect to such an extent that this degree of control is feasible. A Raja Yogi can be in the midst of a situation of intense disturbance, yet remain so unshakeably calm that the inner strength becomes a solace and inspiration to others lacking in that strength. The weak soul is like a leaf at the mercy of the storm; the strong one is a rock in the face of a tempestuous sea.

THE INTERACTIVE SELF

The mountaineer baulks at the size and complexity of the mountain. The sheerness of the western face fills him with apprehension. He has all of the equipment necessary, the boots, spikes, ropes, and harness. He has the know-how that has been acquired from many climbs, but inside his head the game begins. Past difficulties and conquests in the form of recorded *sanskars* battle with each other for space on the screen of the mind. Thoughts coloured by emotions alternate between fear and determination as they are thrown up one after the other. The intellect fights to choose between the oscillating flow of thoughts: Should I go ahead or draw back? I have done this many times before; this is just another peak. But, the last time, I felt my nerve going on a very similar climb? Can I do it?

Finally the choice is made. The intellect decides to move the body towards the base of the steep first section. Drawing on *sanskars* of courage and experience the mountaineer starts to move inexorably towards the top.

This is not just the story of the climbing of a physical mountain. The peak of my highest consciousness looms before me. I have the know-how recorded in me as *sanskars*. After all, my highest state of consciousness is only another way of saying my original state. I have been there before! To get there again however, I have to use the tools of my mind — the boots, spikes, ropes, and harness of my thoughts and emotions. Through the intellect I perceive the height of my goal. Using the know–how and the tools and keeping doubts at a distance, I move towards my aim.

THE INNER GAME

It is rather like a game in which there are two sides and a field. The field in this case is the mind, but such a field which feels the movements of the players. The two sides are the *sanskars* and the intellect. The players on the side of the *sanskars* are habits, beliefs, memories, tendencies, instincts and personality traits, while the intellect has judgement, discernment, the power of memory, decision, understanding, willpower and so on.

If I am weak, my *sanskars* dominate the game, using all possible tricks to overpower my intellect. The intellect's players are without power and don't really know how to play properly. The intellect says to itself: Well, my habits and tendencies have won so many games in the past. Just one more won't make much difference to the result. They always win.

If the *sanskars* were a fair team, then all would be fine. The problem is they are full of impurities and defects and every time they score, the intellect is weakened. Meanwhile the mind is experiencing the whole game, and the emotions, feelings, thoughts and so on come and go according to the quality of the game.

If I really want to have peace of mind, it is not just a question of clearing it of all thoughts (i.e. all players). No doubt I will get some relief. But after the attention of keeping the mind free from thoughts is withdrawn, the same players that were there before return without having been changed in any way.

Similarly if I clear the field and replace the players of the *sanskars* and intellect by a *mantra* (incantation of some sacred syllables), candle-flame or any other form of concentration, I will no doubt experience mental ease but, as soon as I withdraw that attention, the same players return without having been changed. The tensions that were there previously also return.

In order to have lasting and unshakeable peace of mind or rather peace in the field of the mind, instead of just a passing experience of tranquillity, I have to change the players so that the game becomes one of perfect harmony. For this the intellect needs power and knowledge so that it can participate effectively in the game. The *sanskars* need to be purified so that all defects and dirty tricks are removed. For this reason, meditation can bring real and permanent peace of mind by filling the intellect with strength and wisdom and purifying the *sanskars*.

When strength and wisdom unite, the result is peace. When I am aware of my true identity (especially if linked mentally with the Supreme Being[4]) power surges into me through the intellect, purifying the *sanskars* and bringing peace to the mind. Even after a few minutes I can notice some transformation in my

---

4 *This type of meditation will be dealt with in more detail in Chapter 3.*

PERSONAL EXPERIENCE

I used to think of peace as being intimately related to the beauty of nature – the play of waves on a beach, the rustle of wind through a forest, the soaring and swooping of gulls; in short, anything removed from the rush and bustle of the city. Alternatively I would associate peace with some physical form of relaxation like headphones plugged into soothing music, a hot bath after a hard day, a brisk walk in the park, etc. After just a few experiences in meditation, tasting my very essence as peace, I realised very quickly how much I had been fooling myself in trying to extract peace from the world around me or even from some physical sensation in my own body.

I started to see physical relaxation as an escape from tension and not a solution for it; and the beautiful scenes of nature now no longer as sources radiating peace. But in fact it was the mere absence of confusion and tension that appealed to me, appealed, because there was something in me which cried out also to be free from conflict. I discovered that small voice or need was only my true nature demanding to be recognised. I saw that neither the body nor nature could give the peace that the soul was yearning for; it had to be tapped from within. Having found it, I have it relatively constantly, whether in the city or countryside, in comfort or discomfort. In the midst of noise and confusion, peace is really my own.

inner players. When concentrating on other tasks or facing other situations, they behave completely harmoniously.

All of the details of the above definitions and understanding becomes extremely important in the practice of meditation. We will now look into this.

MEDITATION

Yoga means a mental connection or union, achieved through remembrance. Wherever the mind is focused, that can be called yoga. Whenever someone or something is remembered, then I am having yoga with that person or thing. At any moment, I am remembering people, places and things of the past or present, or I am imagining future events. I am continually using this power within as I live in the world outside, trying to find and maintain peace and happiness. I like to remember pleasant experiences and to entertain them as thoughts. I become lost in thought, detached from my immediate surroundings and problems. It is the soul's natural ability to withdraw into itself in the face of external difficulties.

The same ability is used in meditation. The intellect, as the receptacle of knowledge, is that which understands and remembers also. Within the soul, the intellect wanders into the past *sanskars;* then, what was initially a decision to remember someone or something, becomes a thought. As long as the intellect remains fixed on the person or thing, the soul experiences its qualities. For example, when I remember a beautiful summer experience of relative peace and quiet, I re-experience the scenes and forget the immediate problem and drift away. If I remember something painful or unpleasant, or someone's faults, the mind is disturbed. The mind experiences different states according to the types of thoughts that arise. The thoughts depend on where the intellect is focused. In short, as is the consciousness so is the experience.

Raja Yoga meditation works entirely on the level of mind, intellect and *sanskars,* rather than focusing on bodily forms, postures or rituals. The first stage in Raja Yoga is to stabilise the self in the pure experience of the inner tranquillity of the soul.

At first, distracting thoughts may come to the mind. To be free from these, I need to train myself not to get involved in a struggle to contain or eradicate them. I have to learn to step away and become an observer as soon as I become aware of them.

Whenever the situation or atmosphere becomes charged with tension, sorrow, or negativity of any sort, I can withdraw immediately into the self and dive deep into the ocean of *sanskars,* picking up the pearls of peace and contentment. I can then come back to that situation feeling refreshed, calm and clear, with the strength to deal with any circumstance that arises. I also have the ability to contribute these qualities to the situation through thoughts, words, actions and vibrations. The process of self-introspection need only take a few moments.

THE PROCESS OF ACTIVATING HIGHER EMOTIONS

Raja Yoga gives the intellect the power to select those positive *sanskars* which lead to the higher emotions, calm and clear thoughts, and the pure desire to enjoy life in such a way that no sorrow is experienced for the self and no sorrow is given to others.

In the initial stages of meditation, I call to the mind and experience *sanskars* which in most people surface only occasionally. They are deeper than the superficial memories of worldly experiences. These are the pure and powerful *sanskars* relating to the eternal nature of the soul. As the soul is not a material energy, but is a metaphysical energy separate from the body, the dualities of the material world do not relate to the deep, inner nature of the soul.

Consciousness has the same property as light, a powerful force with distinct qualities, yet having no gravitational mass. In fact, the only pull or burden on the soul is the result of its own impure thoughts and negative actions.

I go more deeply than these superficial *sanskars* and perceive the innate qualities of the soul; peace, purity, power and so on. When these original *sanskars* are experienced, love and happiness are also experienced automatically. After some practice, I can have the intellectual power to activate these *sanskars* consciously in daily life at any time. In a situation which would lead most people to experience negative moods or emotions such as fear, depression, anxiety, boredom, fatigue, hatred or aggression, I can become detached and access my innate qualities.

This of course is beneficial not only for me but also for others around me.

THE FIRST STEPS IN MEDITATION

As a soul I must first be aware of my own capacities to sense, discriminate and understand, in order to attune these powers to the proper degree of subtlety and precision. With the physical eyes I can see only gross, material things. It requires a different kind of vision or outlook to see what concerns the non–material, all those experiences which transcend this physical level of existence.

Raja Yoga meditation involves the development and refinement of the so called *third eye* so that I not only see spiritually but also understand and adjust to it in the most natural way possible.

THE USE OF POSITIVE THOUGHTS

There is a common impression that meditation means to empty the mind of all thoughts in order to experience the stillness of the spirit. The mind is not to blame for our existential distress. It is really only a screen upon which thoughts are projected. Its waywardness is due to the quality of thoughts that arise and not some problem inherent in the mind itself.

> If I have positive thoughts, I go in a positive direction. If I have negative thoughts, I move in a negative direction. If I have no thoughts, I go nowhere.

Though this emptying of the mind may bring temporary relief, it's not a natural part of living to have no thoughts. Instead, the mind has to be trained to create the types of thoughts that lead to harmony. Thus, each session of Raja Yoga meditation can be seen as one of thought-training in a similar way to a tennis player who, seeking proficiency, practises his serve, back–hand and volley in order to improve them.

Meditation is the journey towards soul-consciousness and god-consciousness guided by the use of the thoughts created in the mind and the deep and inner memory of the original and innate state of being. I first have to withdraw my attention from all outer circumstances and direct it within towards inner dialogue.

I consider and experience as intimately as possible the thoughts related to the real nature of the self, its role and relationship with the Supreme Being. All such thoughts carry a distinctly positive vibration and lead me to fulfilment.

THE BENEFITS OF OPEN-EYED MEDITATION.

One of the special characteristics of Raja Yoga meditation is that I learn to meditate with my eyes open. The training of thoughts towards a positive bias helps me in facing not only my daily routine, but specifically, in dealing with unexpected situations that tax my real power. Mastering the art of meditating with my eyes open can be of immense value to me in my practical life.

If I restrict myself to seated meditation with my eyes closed, then I am prevented from continuing the meditative experience in the course of my normal activities i.e. walking, eating, moving around and so on.

Meditation is at the same time an incredibly relaxing experience as well as a heightening of perception powers and reaction response. In this way, I can be walking along the street in a meditative state and yet have a very quick perception and reaction response to the surrounding pedestrians and traffic.

SUMMARY

These are the major points in this chapter:

✪ The answer to the question, Who am I? is: I am the soul, the living and intelligent inner being. I inhabit and give life to the body. The body is the means through which I, the soul, express myself and experience the world around me.

✪ The soul is neither male nor female.

✪ When I assume my true identity as a spiritual being, then I also immediately have access to the love, peace, happiness and power that are more than just qualities. They are part of me.

✪ Just as the driver in a car sits behind the wheel with the steering wheel in his hands, the soul sits in a specific point in the centre of the brain near the pineal body.

✪ The soul is seen as an infinitesimal point of conscient light.

✪ In meditation attention is first directed as follows: I am the soul, a tiny point of conscious light energy, centred in the spot between the brows.

✪ The intrinsic or innate qualities of the soul are peace, love, happiness, truth, power, purity and balance.

✪ The soul functions through three main faculties: mind, intellect and *sanskars*. Together they produce the state of the individual at any one moment.

✪ If I have positive thoughts, I go in a positive direction. If I have negative thoughts, I move in a negative direction. If I have no thoughts, I go nowhere.

✪ Meditation is a process of bringing forth higher emotions through understanding, and bringing under control the inner processes of the self.

✪ If I master the art of meditating with my eyes open, this art can be of immense value to me in my practical life.

(M.C. Escher Hand With Reflecting Sphere, Lithograph (National Gallery of Art, Washington))

Chapter 2

Thought and consciousness

One of the most important areas of consideration in human life is that of relationships. Of these the first and most fundamental one is the one I have with myself. How well do I know myself? Am I my own friend? If I think over the last week or month, how many of my reactions were unexpected or uncontrolled? How many left me perplexed, confused or even depressed?

If there have been several such situations, it's an indication that there are still things deep within me that I have not discovered or come to terms with. Normally a friend is someone whose company I enjoy, for whom there is love and from whom there is some benefit. But am I a friend to myself? If not, it may be simply because I don't know my own depths.

The door that opens to the world of spiritual knowledge and inculcation of positive qualities is the consciousness, 'I am an eternal soul'. If I understand and experience its implications, I can still my restless mind and create the stability necessary to absorb spirituality and power. I can channel the potential for good that I have within myself just as a river, when properly harnessed, provides water for the lives of many.

It's obvious that I have to spend a great part of each day involved in situations born from my roles, routines, responsibilities and relationships. If I am not careful these very aspects of my life in the world may absorb my energy totally — just as a battery discharges. I need to find time to recharge myself. The peace and happiness I require

internally come from understanding and knowing the self.
By concentrating on the atom, scientists have unleashed the power within it. Similarly, by concentrating lovingly on the soul and its eternal bond to the Supreme Soul, I can unleash my own potential and pure power.

The main points to be covered in this chapter are:
- ✪ the state of the soul and its relationship to the world;
- ✪ understanding the nature of consciousness;
- ✪ the two basic types of consciousness – 'I, the soul' and 'I, the body';
- ✪ the three regions of existence– physical, subtle and incorporeal;
- ✪ the quality of thoughts;
- ✪ the five types of thought – waste, negative, necessary, ordinary and elevated;
- ✪ how thoughts create an atmosphere.

STATE OF THE SOUL – STATE OF THE WORLD

One of the concepts that arises from the present intense search to redefine the individual and his/her relationship with society is that of holism. It comes from the Greek root *holos* meaning *the whole*. It refers basically to a world view that takes into account the interconnectedness of all things within a given system.

Applied to the question of health, for example, it is an integral approach to understanding illness and its causes and prevention. It reflects the necessity of understanding human beings as *whole* persons and not as a collection of organs. In other words : body, mind and soul. Environmental, social, physical, mental and spiritual factors all contribute to our health.

STATE	QUALITIES OF HEALTH
Self	Love, peace, happiness, truth, power
Mind	Positivity, harmony, balance, discipline
Body	Disease-free, vitality, balance
Relationships	Harmony, respect, sincerity
Society	Order, co-operation, justice, tolerance
Environment	Cleanliness, harmony, balance

This more encompassing world view has its roots in antiquity. The ancient Indians, Chinese and Greeks all saw the state of health as the balance between all the above factors. Curiously, the word *therapist* comes from the name of a group of Essene monks who sought the cure of the soul through a life of contemplation.

Even though the World Health Organisation defines health in terms of our mental, physical and social well-being, the absolute interconnectedness of even these three, in the sense of how they affect each other, is generally unacknowledged. The starting and end points of the process – the state of the self and that of the environment respectively – have been omitted.

If we simply made a list of six states (the above five and that of relationships) as seen in the left column of the diagram (p. 36), we might not immediately see the interdependence between them. By jotting down a few aspects that would qualify as a healthy state of each one of them (right column), how they affect each other becomes self-evident.

Just as it's hard to imagine a truly healthy body without a healthy mind, the extent of the effect that each of the states has on all the others is just as encompassing. In other words, the state of the environment or of society has to do with all the other states.

Look at the following diagram:

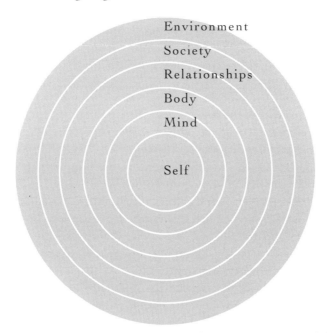

The seed of both the problems and the solutions is the state of the self. To change the self is to change the world.

In order to do that the first step is to understand the nature of consciousness.

WHAT IS CONSCIOUSNESS?

Consciousness essentially refers to the fact that the soul has awareness of its own existence. It's what is behind the thought 'I exist' or 'I am'. Usually, together with this affirmation, there is a further addition — I am something or someone. This addition can be called the self-identity. It affects the way consciousness works. Since what I feel myself to be generally doesn't remain stable, the state of consciousness is always fluctuating.

In one moment I may have the consciousness, 'I am a man' or 'I am a woman', and in the next, 'I am an engineer' or 'I am a doctor' or 'I am an American' or 'I am a German'. On a deeper level I can be in the consciousness, 'I am a soul, a child of God.'

If I examine any thought-decision-action process, I will find that behind it, there is always the feeling: I am something or the other. Consciousness is the springboard for thought, decisions and actions. In other words, the soul reacts to external circumstances according to whatever it feels itself to be at that particular moment.

For example, a surgeon is able to perform surgery when there is the consciousness of being a surgeon. That very consciousness unlocks or gives the soul access to all the information and experience related to being a surgeon.

My state of consciousness affects my mental state, attitude and vision and ultimately the actions I perform and the situations in which I find myself. If I want to transform all of the other things, I first have to change my state of consciousness.

The two basic categories of consciousness relate either to the soul or to the body.

SOUL-CONSCIOUSNESS – THE ORIGIN OF VIRTUES

The innate qualities of the soul (as described in the previous chapter) are also what can be termed the original *sanskars*. When I am aware of my true identity as a soul, these qualities become accessible.

In the consciousness 'I, the soul', I perceive the limiting nature of the ego. Instead of observing others as functions of my own needs, I begin to see how everyone exists in his/her own right. By tuning into my own innate qualities, it's as if I get into a frequency that makes others comfortable by allowing them to be what they intrinsically are. When my vision is focused on these core values in others, they become common denominators which link me to them. Bridges replace what previously were walls.

Many of us may have experienced the difference between travelling on a road full of pot-holes without any suspension and doing the same trip with the shock-absorbers in place. Since the majority of aspects of our lives are fixed, such as the body we have, our parents and children and so on, virtues certainly make the journey on the road of life much more comfortable.

THE DIFFERENCE BETWEEN
SOUL-CONSCIOUSNESS AND BODY-CONSCIOUSNESS

IN SOUL-CONSCIOUSNESS	IN BODY-CONSCIOUSNESS
I am free.	I am in bondage.
I can understand everything that I do.	I have many questions and few answers.
I know I am eternal; so I have no fear of death.	I am afraid of dying (losing the body).
I am able to practise self-control.	I have no control over the sense organs.
I am able to maintain enthusiasm.	I become bored and depressed easily.
I can mentally fly beyond the body.	The wings of the soul are clipped.
The intellect is sharp.	The intellect is dull.
I can travel mentally to regions beyond this world.	I am limited to the perception of this world.
The past, present and future of my part can be seen more clearly.	I see a distorted past and have no clear aim for the future.
I know that real beauty is of the soul.	I am disturbed by feelings of attraction to the physical beauty of bodies.
I spread the fragrance of virtues.	I give sorrow, like a thorn pricking others.
I respect all individuals and relate to them with humility.	I see everyone relative to my identity; my life revolves totally around me.
I am aware of my own innate qualities and those of others.	My vision is fixed on my own and others' defects.
I can achieve better results with less effort.	There is more effort and less result, which leads to tension and tiredness.

THE LIMITS OF 'I, THE BODY'

Much of my internal struggle is between what I really am and what I think I am. If, as the conscious and eternal energy called *soul,* I insist on identifying myself with the finite body, I am in for some trouble. It's like trying to put a big foot into a small shoe — it hurts! In the consciousness, 'I the body', I have to make countless compensations to accommodate myself in the bodily shoe.

By identifying myself exclusively with the fleeting attractions and connections of the physical form, it seems that I must pay for them with discomfort and spiritual insecurity and eventually pain. The consciousness: 'I am so-and-so, the child of so-and-so, the resident of such-and-such a place, of this or that religion or race, of such a profession, age and so on', sets the parameters for the ego to play around in.

Being limited, I become busy with the senses and their objects in an attempt to cover up the basic deception that they pose. 'We can give you whatever you need', they seem to say, as a myriad of illusions take birth. The reality of my greater spiritual existence is forgotten and a temporary reality automatically creates its order of priorities. This inverts the deeper innate values and brings insecurity. I become trapped in a world of duality, of likes and dislikes.

As the actor-soul I am not the costume (body) nor really the role I am playing. The 'I, the body' consciousness or body-consciousness, for short, doesn't only restrict me to the form but to the name as well. While I remain a prisoner of my own roles, I can't see the wider aspects of the drama of life in which I am involved. I am confined to the conditions of each place, moment and circumstance, and tied up in the bonds of past habits and attitudes. If the situation harmonises with my expectations, I feel good. If not, I feel dejected and search for ways to escape from the imaginary or real threats that the situation presents. In this manner, I pass from one scene to another, like a piece of cork on the high seas at the mercy of the waves of circumstance.

The soul in body-consciousness cannot control its own movements, but they are imposed by external conditions, which the soul itself is continually determining according to the law of cause and effect (see chapter 4).

PERSONAL EXPERIENCE

I used to think that everything was unreal or an illusion but, after going into it deeply, I realised that the drama of life, the stage of the world, the actors and the roles are real enough. I concluded that my vision of things, and therefore my deductions, can be illusory or not.

The basic illusion, 'I am this body', was a thread running through my existence. Upon this illusion all other thoughts, decisions and actions were strung.

BODY-CONSCIOUSNESS –
THE ORIGIN OF NEGATIVITY

When I have inner strength, my tendencies and talents are reflected in the form of virtues. If the self is weak, those same tendencies emerge as vices. Vices are just virtues that have lost their direction and power.

The clearest example of this is love. When it is radiating from a strong self, it is unlimited, unconditional and retains respect for everything and everyone. The same love from a weakened soul tends to confine itself to limits. I get imprisoned in relationships of attachment. I run after objects and objectives in the form of greed. I become stuck to my self-image in the form of vanity or arrogance. In a sense, if power and understanding are removed from the virtues, they themselves become the vices.

In this state of spiritual insecurity the six main negative forces or vices are born:

- ✪ ATTACHMENT – the attempt to find security through developing relationship of ownership or possessiveness with people and objects;
- ✪ GREED – the attempt to find fulfilment through the acquisition of material goods, position or status, or through the physical senses as with food;
- ✪ EGO – the cultivation of a self-image that is false, temporary or unreal;
- ✪ LUST – the urge towards sense satisfaction as a means of fulfilment;
- ✪ ANGER – the feeling of animosity when any of the other vices are threatened;
- ✪ LAZINESS – the urge towards inactivity on a spiritual, mental or physical level when the demand is otherwise.

The underlying cause of the poor health of our individual and collective world is body-consciousness and its manifestation through these six negativities and their progeny.

The basis of sexual, racial, social and religious prejudice that I may have is the vision and classification of others as their respective bodies, cultures or social customs. I understand that it is the ignorance of our true nature that breeds prejudice, that generates conflict, that gives rise to war and hatred and so on. The so called vicious cycle continues until the seed of ignorance is removed.

Body-consciousness is basically attachment to my physical self-image. I become trapped in the world of names and forms and limit myself to the conditions of the place, time and circumstances that are surrounding me.

SOUL-CONSCIOUS VISION

How I see others is definitely based on the consciousness with which I view myself. So many different possibilities of perception arise when I have to deal with others. Many times I don't even see individuals as they really are, but merely as part of their national, cultural or racial background. Age, sex, profession, social status and degree of beauty add to the compartments that become subtle or obvious barriers in my relationships with them. They camouflage my own self-identity and tint the glasses through which I observe, and therefore, react to others.

If I replace all of these categories with the vision of the soul as a tiny dot of conscious energy as distinct from the physical body ·and all its identifying attributes, it brings a great sense of freedom. I can move away from all prejudice in a very effective way.

Different results are attained according to the level of awareness. The following example is that of a boss towards his/her employees:

	BODY-CONSCIOUSNESS	SOUL-CONSCIOUSNESS
AWARENESS	I am the boss here; I know more than everyone here. After all, that's why I am the boss.	I am a spiritual being. I have to play out a role of responsibility. Each of my employees has his/her own specific role.
THOUGHT	They should listen to me. After all I am the one who pays their salaries.	Let me listen to their suggestions. Perhaps we can improve something.
DECISION	I will show them who is boss here.	Let me understand each of their specialities.
ACTION	The boss shouts and argues with them.	A two-way dialogue ensues.
RESULT	Ill-feeling between boss and employees.	Respect and a climate of trust is maintained.

ACTORS, COSTUMES AND ROLES

It's not a question of dealing with these bodily classifications one by one, through analysis and reason. I simply need to experiment with the idea that: 'I, the soul, a point of spiritual energy, am here to play a role through this particular body. I, the soul, came into it at one point and, when it has served its purpose, I will leave it. Other people are also souls playing roles through their bodies and are subject to the same ground-rules as I am.'

When I speak or interact with them, I must try to remember this spiritual truth and not be influenced by bias or bigotry owing to any physical classifications. Before we are male, female, black, white, Indian or American, Muslim or Christian, we are spiritual beings who, according to our respective pasts, find ourselves in these bodies, with different roles to play.

My body-costume could have been a different colour, gender or nationality. For various good reasons, I the actor, am playing my role in this particular costume. The awareness that the actor, role and costume are separate, but connected, brings a sense of inner detachment. I start to pay more attention to the way I am playing my role and enjoy it more. I am able to determine the quality of emotions rather than let them take over. I can't change others but I can determine the quality of the role that I play and tune in with whatever each situation requires me to do.

When I use the word *my,* I can be referring to *my* mind, *my* body, *my* relationships or *my* world. However, I can't really say *my being* or *my soul,* because that is what I am. According to the interdependence of the mind and the self I affect my mind and my mind affects me. In other words: I create my thoughts which inevitably come back to me.

THE QUALITY OF THOUGHTS

As we have seen, the types of thoughts and the state of the body affect each other mutually. Think of the last time you had a bad headache and you'll probably agree. Less obvious is the fact that our very thoughts are involved in creating the headache.

Equally, the type of food we ingest causes some effect in our mind. We can immediately see the effect of a strong pain-killing drug on our minds. It slows down the thinking process itself. Less obvious is the effect our thoughts have on the food we prepare and the things we make. The effect is always bilateral.

For this reason the possibility of getting caught up in vicious cycles is ever-present, exactly because of the mutual dependence of all the states — self, mind, body, relationships, society and environment. If I am weak or negative, this affects my thoughts and everything else. When I look at the state of my own personal world, I see the reflections of my inner state in everything.

THE FIVE TYPES OF THOUGHTS

As has already been shown, the quality of thoughts that I grant entry into the mind definitely affects my mental state and therefore my experience in meditation. It's reasonable to expect that if I spend 23 hours in a state of mental abandon without any effort towards self-checking, then the hour that I set aside for my meditation experience will be anything but powerful.

Regular meditation practice brings change and benefit to my family, work and social life. Attention on the types of thoughts that I am cultivating during the course of my activities will enhance that practice.

There are various categories into which thoughts fall:

✪ WASTE THOUGHTS — those that have nothing to do with reality. This can include things like the doubts, excuses, the creation and continuance of unrealistic fantasies ('building castles in the air'), worry about trivialities, confusion, misunderstandings and paranoia.

- ✪ NEGATIVE THOUGHTS — those that have their origin in the vices such as anger, greed, ego, lust, attachment, laziness or any one of their many progeny.
- ✪ NECESSARY THOUGHTS — those connected with the exercise of one's family, professional, social or other responsibilities. This could include the responsibility of looking after one's health and hygiene.
- ✪ ORDINARY THOUGHTS — those associated with mundane matters, news and views about situations.
- ✪ ELEVATED THOUGHTS — those related to meditative introspection, the contemplation on aspects of spiritual knowledge or self-development and spiritual service of others – real creative thinking.

HOW THOUGHTS CREATE THE ATMOSPHERE

The word *atmosphere* has two meanings. One refers to the physical air around us and the other to the more subtle aspects that thought vibrations create in a particular space. No one can deny that the atmosphere of a crowded bar is different from that of a church. This is mainly because of the effect of different types of thoughts and feelings in that space. Even someone deaf and blind would have the ability to pick up the difference.

Sound vibrations are invisible but their impact isn't. A pneumatic drill or a jet breaking the sound barrier jolt both our minds and the walls of our houses. Thought vibrations can't be seen but their impact is even more pervasive. The panic that people generate during a tragedy or the euphoria of victory in a championship game of football are examples of how thoughts create an atmosphere.

On a subtler level, many of us have the experience of rudimentary telepathy – 'Oh! I was just thinking of you and you called'. Thoughts connect individuals over large distances. Doctors inform us that over 90% of the body's illnesses have a psychosomatic origin. That makes the human body the prime example of how thoughts affect matter.

Since the world is made up of the collective, personal worlds of all individuals, then it's easy to see how the international political, economic and social atmosphere is nothing more than the collective effects of all our thoughts.

BIRTH, DEATH AND REBIRTH

The realisation of the self as a soul, an eternal entity, naturally leads to the questions:

- ✪ Where is the soul before it comes into a physical body?
- ✪ Where does the soul go after it leaves it?
- ✪ What is the purpose of eternity?

These are questions that have deeply concerned us throughout history. Most accept that there is some ordered purpose to the play of creation but, viewing it through the spectacles of body-consciousness, I cannot see that purpose, as I am imprisoned by present needs, plans and desires. As the time of death of the body approaches, I almost instinctively begin considering the idea of life after death.

I subconsciously know that I am a soul. Birth, life, death and rebirth are just stages of existence. All natural processes can be found to have a beginning, a middle, an end and a new beginning to continue the cycle. The soul takes a bodily form, gives life to it, and after a period of time, longer or shorter, leaves it and takes another, suited to the continuation of its role.

As long as the soul is in the body, the body grows like a plant, from small to large, from baby to child, from youth to maturity. It then begins to decay and finally becomes unusable. The moment that the soul leaves, the body becomes like a dead log. It immediately starts to decompose and eventually goes back into the dust. Again the soul moves into a tiny baby's body, in the womb of a new mother. After some time it emerges as a newborn baby and immediately begins to manifest the same mind, intellect and *sanskars* it has carried with it from its previous life. It is the same soul but in a new physical situation.

Thus death is merely the means by which a complete change of circumstances and environment for the soul takes place. Time never kills the soul, but the body, being a part of nature or matter, obeys the law of entropy[5] which states that everything new becomes old and eventually ceases to hold its form. The molecular components of this body disintegrate only to re-integrate as another form some time later.

The process of birth–life–death–rebirth is also eternal. It has always gone on and will continue. The soul comes into the body, expresses a role and experiences the results of that expression through it for a certain time period, then leaves it, and the process starts again.

Similarly, souls come into this world, remain here as actors for a number of lifetimes and then return to the region from which they came, where they abide for a period of rest. The process also starts again. The souls again come into action. The pattern is a cyclic one.

THE THREE REGIONS OF EXISTENCE

If I make a complete regression back to my start I will arrive at a moment

PERSONAL EXPERIENCE

Whenever I have had to go to a funeral, especially those in which the body lies in state for all to see and touch, I have wondered at the silent awe in which most people remain. The new absence of a loved one is staring us all in the face as we reflect on the impermanence of our own bodies. I never could embrace the image of a fiery hell or heavenly, blissful world beyond the clouds. The idea of living forever, tormented in a sulphurous pit or conversely, savouring a life of perpetual bliss in a fairytale kingdom, seem so far removed from reality. Through the experience of meditation I have discovered that it is a much more natural process when stripped of myth and mystery.

---

5   *From the Second Law of Thermodynamics which states that energy, when in use, moves from a state of availability to one of non-availability, i.e. it gets used up.*

in which I was not present in this physical world – having no contact with it, no relationships nor even thoughts about anything. I was beyond, not in the sense of physical distance, but certainly in a dimension that transcends this one of time and space.

To give greater meaning to where I am, I need to understand where I've come from. The following are the characteristics of three distinct regions or vibratory fields that make up our reality:

(12th Century European map of the world)

> *Just as some previous civilisations believed the Earth to be flat, in a similar way, there are other subtler aspects to our living here that our senses haven't a hope of coming close to.*

PHYSICAL REGION

It's difficult to imagine that the planet where we live out our lives is at this moment whizzing through space at the most astounding velocity as it adjusts itself to even greater physical forces in the universe. Our limited sense perception makes everything appear to be still, and also gives rise to the illusion that the Earth is flat! In a similar way, there are other subtler aspects to our living here that our senses haven't a hope of coming close to. To understand what is beyond here, I need to go beyond the senses. Paradoxically, it's only when I comprehend what transcends the physical that I can truly come to terms with it.

The physical universe is a stage of action where human souls descend into physical bodies to play out their respective parts in a drama of unimaginable proportions. Time, space, matter, movement and sound are the salient characteristics of the physical universe which is governed by well-defined physical, chemical and biological laws.

This world is a vast amphitheatre of action in which embodied souls play their respective and variety roles. In India, the world which human beings inhabit is called *karma kshetra* (the field of action) because it is here that people sow the seeds of actions and reap the fruit. It is here that the soul takes on a body of flesh and bones and expresses the role that it has latent within itself.

There is a direct relationship between the acting out of each soul's role and the state of matter. On this immense stage of deserts, forests, mountains and seas, illuminated by the sun, moon and stars, the drama of existence is enacted. In the drama, we actor-souls are subject to dualities, ranging from pleasure to pain, birth to death, purity to impurity, happiness to sorrow, new to old, positive to negative; the vast pageant of history crawls along as time inexorably devours all. As souls change, history changes and matter or nature itself moves through different states to accompany those changes.[6]

There are two other dimensions beyond the limits of this vast expanse of the physical solar system and galaxies. They are regions of non-material light and cannot be reached by any physical means because it is simply not a question of light years or kilometres. They are regions which transcend the physical plane and therefore can only be experienced through divine vision, perceivable to the third eye. Through deep meditation I can travel to these regions and experience the bliss of being free from the limits of body-consciousness. The only means I have to experiment with them is thought.

INCORPOREAL REGION

There is a vague yet recurring memory of a place or region above and beyond anything we can see, touch or feel here. When trying to remember God or the Supreme Being, members of the major religions will generally close their eyes and then try to send their thoughts to somewhere up there.

This indicates the existence of a region above and beyond which is connected with a supreme energy in some way. The place that Christians refer to as *Heaven*, or the Hindus as *Shantidham* (the abode of peace) or *Paramdham* (the Supreme Abode) and the Buddhists as *Nirvana* (*nir* – beyond, *vana* – sound) appear to be all one and the same. In Raja Yoga it is simply termed the *home of souls* or *soul world*.

The basic characteristics of the soul world are stillness (no matter) and silence (no sound). In deep meditation this region is experienced as a reddish-golden light which is totally unlike physical light.

As this is the home of souls, we remain completely free in this light-element in a latent state until the moment comes when we have to appear in the physical region. Before I came to the earth, I was here with all other souls, my brothers. The experience of complete and utter peace, purity and silence is here in my sweet home. Here I am totally untainted by matter. I abide here in the incorporeal form as a starlike point of light. I remain dormant, with my roles in the physical world merged or latent within me.

From this place I come into the womb of the mother and stay with that

6 *More about this in volume 2.*

*The three worlds or regions:
the physical region, the subtle region
and the soul world.*

particular body until accident, sickness or old age determine that the body is no longer fit to be used. At that moment I leave it to take on another body-costume.

In this way the population here continually grows, with souls coming into new roles and bodies from two sources:

✪ new souls are constantly coming from the soul-world;

✪ the souls that are already here leave bodies and take on new ones in a process that is called death and rebirth or reincarnation.[7]

SUBTLE REGION

There is also an intermediate region between the physical and the incorporeal, that can be called the *subtle region*. Its function is to help in the renewal of the processes in the physical region.

At this present time in history this subtle plane is serving as a place for visions and messages in order to accelerate the process of transformation. It's like a cocoon in which the physical region is undergoing its metamorphosis. Because the process is relatively long and thorough, the majority of human beings don't even realise that it's already happening. However, some individuals and groups here and there are aware of the positive transforming influence of the subtle region at this time.

Its basic characteristic is the existence of light images without sound or matter. Visual scenes can be observed and thoughts transmitted but, as its name suggests, the scenes are subtle and therefore non-physical. Sometimes it is called the *angelic region*.

THE ORIGINAL STATE OF THE SOUL

The experience of the original state in which my innate qualities are at their fullest potential is recorded in me as my original *sanskars*. It is this fundamental experience that we have always sought to get back to. I am originally a star-like point of perfect peace, twinkling in the golden-red expanse of the soul world. I am fully charged with spiritual energy which naturally manifests as

7 *More about this in chapter 4*

love, joy, peace and purity when I first come into this physical world.

Over the period of many births, I have gradually become attached to the senses and their various objects and have forgotten my original attributes. My ability to harmonise with matter has been supplanted by matter's control over me.

If I practise contemplation on my original nature, and live and do everything with the realisation that I am a soul and not a body, then these original qualities reappear naturally. They are my basic attributes. To seek them outside me is just like the musk deer running after the sweet smell of musk, unaware that it is coming from its own navel. Peace of mind is my own property. It automatically flows from within me once I am soul-conscious.

The original *sanskars* are within me. I only have to let them become thoughts and keep them flowing. Whatever thoughts are in my mind, that is the state I experience. Soul-conscious thoughts bring peace of mind. Body-conscious thoughts disturb me. It is I who decide what state of mind to experience. I can either be the natural essence of peace, or in a state of turmoil. I have the power of decision; the situations do not decide for me.

When I am far away from my home and loved ones, it's a common experience to have a nostalgic feeling that brings a lump to the throat just thinking about it. A lot of what we have been doing for the last couple of thousand years has been motivated by a type of spiritual home-sickness that impels us to create paths of search that have the declared or undeclared aim of returning to that state variously termed as 'merging with the light', 'God's bosom', 'back to the source' and so on.

The memory of the freedom and peace of the original state is indelibly impressed on every single soul. That's why there are so many basic similarities between the different traditions of spiritual pursuit. Meditation serves to activate those original qualities. Quite literally, the distance that separates me from the experience of my home is one thought.

RAJA YOGA MEDITATION -
REGAINING THE AWARENESS

In meditation it's not necessary to empty the mind of thought. I use my most natural endowment of thinking as a take-off point into the consciousness of the true self. I climb up a well-prepared ladder of thoughts and eventually leave that ladder and am immersed in the pure experience of what I really am.

Reflecting on the vast field of pure and real thoughts can occupy me for quite long periods of time. First comes the realisation: I am the soul, I am the mind, intellect and *sanskars*. My ears, eyes, nose, mouth and skin are just the organs through which I can enjoy the experience of life. It is due to body-consciousness and the build-up of past negative *sanskars* that I have remained imprisoned by certain habits and tendencies.

I can even picture myself trapped in the cage of the body, but I am the soul.

With the speed of a thought I can detach and fly away like a bird to the soul world, where I can easily experience my original state.

During the initial stages of meditation many wasteful thoughts do come. This is due to my long-standing habit of thinking aimlessly. The mind has been attracted or repelled by so many things. I have been buffeted from one experience to another, one scene to another. I must break the negative cycles of worry, doubt and confusion within by recharging myself with my own original attributes of peace, purity, love, joy and bliss. I must make sure the engines of my senses are not burning up the vital fuel of inner peace.

Raja Yoga meditation is the means by which I can achieve the right use of thought energy and channel it into controlling my moods. It means to turn my thoughts away from those of anger, greed and frustration to a far higher level of peace and contentment.

CONTROLLING THE FLOW OF THOUGHTS

Before doing any action I first have to think; yet how much time do I spend developing the thinking faculty, the mind? With knowledge of the power of thought and soul-consciousness, I can remove inner storms by exercising control over any mood which confronts me at any moment. As such, the continuing spiritual education that meditation affords me brings enormous benefits both to myself and to all others with whom I have contact. Meditation is a continuing experience rather than a static one done at a certain time of the day.

Through the practice of soul-consciousness and meditation, I can remain strong and contented internally, come what may. I am a soul and I have my own store of peace from which I can draw at any time. I can draw on my own experience of just being a soul wherever I am, in the countryside or city, at home or at work.

Very simply and naturally, I, the soul, on the wings of my thoughts, can fly to my eternal and highest home and experience my own original attributes. As I begin to practise soul-consciousness, I learn to detach myself from the diverse and difficult situations around me and turn naturally to my spiritual home. The mind becomes automatically controlled by this flow of peace. With the fundamental understanding of the distinctions between soul and body, the spiritual and the physical, I begin to meditate.

SUMMARY

- ✪ Just as the body has many organs and limbs, the soul has the subtle faculties of thinking power (mind), reasoning power (intellect) and *sanskars,* or personality traits, which are the basis of individual uniqueness.

- ✪ The essential functions of the mind are thought, desire, feeling, emotion, imagination, ideation and sensation.

- ✪ The intellect's basic functions are decision-making, reasoning power, will power, judgement, discrimination power, remembrance and the ability to understand, know and recognise.

- ✪ *Sanskars* take the form of habits, tendencies, personality traits, memories, values, beliefs, learning, talents and instincts.

- ✪ The process of the self is cyclic. From the *sanskars* arise thoughts which are then processed by the intellect to decide whether to carry the thought into action or not. The experience of the action is recorded in the soul as a *sanskar.*

- ✪ The state of the soul affects the mind, body, relationships, society and ultimately the state of the world. To change the self is to change the world.

- ✪ There are five categories of thoughts — waste, negative, necessary, ordinary and elevated. The quality of the thoughts creates the subtle atmosphere.

- ✪ Consciousness refers to the fact that the soul has awareness of its own existence.

- ✪ There are two basic categories of consciousness — that of the soul and that of the body. Soul-consciousness opens the doors to the world of spirituality and allows the natural development of virtues. Body-consciousness is the origin of negativity or vices.

- ✪ Soul-consciousness is food for the mind that strengthens the intellect and keeps the individual beyond the influence of negativity.

- ✪ There are six main negative traits — attachment, greed, ego, lust, anger and laziness.

- ✪ There are three regions of existence — the physical universe of time, space, sound and movement, the subtle region and the incorporeal world which is the home of souls.

In all cultures and religions there is some special memorial or ritual in which light is always allied to what is holy or sacred. It is a reminder of the form of God as light.

Chapter 3
God, the missing connection

The highest achievement of my inner pilgrimage is to reach God. On our journey towards betterment some of us consciously search for truth, others for love and still others for beauty. If these three aspects — love, truth and beauty — were offered as those which most summarise God's qualities, there would be few willing to argue.

Unfortunately just as the word God has been so much used and abused out of context, love, truth and beauty have all but lost their deeper meanings.

Love has been misinterpreted, confused and misused in so many different ways. Many varieties of falsehoods masquerade as truths. Beauty has come to be associated with the temporary and ephemeral. Even so, the love, truth and beauty that epitomise God do not have substitutes and so the search has continued.

The love we have between us as members of the same world family is inconstant and conditional. What I feel is true today is discredited tomorrow. Physical beauty is easily disfigured. If I have been searching for a love that never lets me down, a truth that is unshakeable and a beauty that goes beyond the superficial, I have indeed been searching for God – perhaps without even knowing it.

In this chapter we will explore the following:

✪ different concepts of God

✪ the instruments to realise God

PERSONAL EXPERIENCE

I used to think of God's infiniteness as vastness. When I started to meditate and go deeply on my inner journey, I realised that physical criteria have nothing to do with God's greatness. For me the one meaning of infinite that started to make more and more sense was that of being beyond geometrical dimensions or infinitesimal, i.e. no size. It became reasonable to see that God can have the same form as human souls since size on a metaphysical level has nothing to do with attributes. The only difference is in the qualities, not in the size. Then came the big discovery — I had rightly thought God to be great, but that doesn't mean He is expanded throughout the entire universe. I understood that, although He may be without a physical body, it doesn't mean that He is formless. In fact I now needed to know exactly what His form was in order to concentrate on it and start to receive His energy.

I used to think that God dwelt in the heart of human beings. Through deep meditation I could see that what I consider to be God within me is really just my eternal and unforgettable impression of that One. His real abode and mine were one and the same —the soul world.

✪ on the metaphysical plane how like attracts like
✪ the nature and identity of God
✪ the acts of God
✪ similarities and differences between the soul and God
✪ meditation as a link of love.

CONCEPTS OF GOD

The word *God* perhaps conjures up in our minds images of some vague yet almighty being or energy. If a survey were to be done among believers throughout the world as to the identity and attributes of God, some of the answers in common would include those shown in the box opposite.

If pressed for further details, the same people would affirm that they do not know who or what God is. Many say that God is beyond our comprehension and the questions remain unanswered:

Where is that One? What is His[8] role? How can I get in contact? What is God's relationship with the Creation? What does God really do? What can I receive from Him?

Even if answers are offered they are rarely such that all human beings could universally identify with.

In polytheistic religions, there is always one God who stands above the others, sometimes with a consort but, nevertheless, the chief among gods. Monotheistic faiths believe God to be one single supreme being. Traditions, sacred texts and monuments, sayings and rituals all over the world point to the existence of, and belief in, one knowing, all-powerful and merciful being. That one is universally prayed to and recognised as the remover of sorrow, the giver of happiness — in short, someone certainly worth knowing.

INSTRUMENTS TO REALISE GOD

Perhaps I have been avoiding coming towards God because of the extraordinary confusion surrounding the subject. The epithets abound — God is everywhere and

---

8 *Editor's note: Though God is neither male nor female, for sake of ease we have preferred to use the conventional He, Him and His as pronouns when referring to God. To use it or its to refer to the Supreme Being would not be appropriate. To use He/She would make the text too complicated but we have included this form here and there to remind the reader of God's neutrality.*

in everything, God and the human soul are one and the same, God is unknowable and so on.

Maybe I have just lacked the tools with which to be able to discover God. The whole universe of things going on within a tiny drop of blood can be instantly revealed by the use of a microscope. In the same way, the secrets behind our realities remain hidden until unearthed by the appropriate instruments. With which tools then, can I perceive God?

That I haven't been able to understand myself is amply demonstrated by the periods of confusion and inner turmoil I go through. Sometimes I don't understand those with whom I share the same room or house, let alone my neighbours next door!

The word *misunderstanding* occurs frequently in my relationships with others. It indicates that the quality of my mind, consciousness or even conscience hasn't been sufficiently clear to establish real rapport between myself and others. The perception and realisation of God remain even further out of reach.

> **IDENTITY AND ATTRIBUTES OF GOD**
>
> The creative principle
>
> All-powerful
>
> All-loving, all-knowing
>
> Absolute Truth
>
> Supreme parent (Mother/Father)
>
> Some form of superior non-physical energy
>
> God is one, morally perfect and absolutely just.
>
> God is the supreme benefactor

There's a very specific methodology involved in firstly understanding and organising myself, and from that, coming to terms with God. As explored in the previous chapter, I already have the most powerful of all instruments, the energy of my own mind, to work with. The extent to which I am able to research into the subject of God-realisation depends on the quality of my thoughts .

LIKE ATTRACTS LIKE

If the quality of my thoughts influences my physical health, the atmosphere around me and my relationships, it will definitely affect my relationship with God. Unlike physics in which like and unlike forces attract each other, the basic principle of spirituality is that like attracts like. If my mind is caught up in the spinning of negativity, the dissimilarity will create distance between myself and God.

The initial experiences of soul-consciousness confirm that the real self has an existence separate from the physical body. With the awareness of being a soul, I begin to have a certain amount of mastery over my own thoughts and their quality The process of finishing negativity is accelerated. Just stepping away from the limited consciousness of the body and bodily connections stops negative thinking in the same way that just by flicking the switch, the lamp is turned on and darkness finishes.

If explorers had never ventured beyond their home countries, they would have remained firm in the belief that the rest of the world simply didn't exist. In the same way, if I allow myself to stay only within the physical and limited sphere of thinking, then I would declare that there is nothing beyond. It is when I make the effort to go outside the confines of my previous thinking, that I have the chance of discovering more.

The quest for a source of love, truth and beauty eventually brings me to the necessity of looking beyond not only my own body, but also other human beings and matter itself. Through the practice of seeing the self as an eternal soul and disciplining my mind I create the possibility of discovering the existence and nature of God and coming close to that One.

NATURE AND IDENTITY OF GOD

It's not too difficult to understand that out of all the billions of souls, there is One who could be designated as the Supreme, because of His perfect love, total truth and absolute beauty.

In order to maintain the concept of constancy, it is reasonable to accept that such an unlimited being is never born from a mother's womb nor undergoes the experience of death. He/She never passes through the stages of growing up nor gets involved in specific relationships with individuals.

Just as the human soul has a mind, intellect and a specific set of *sanskars* that determine each one's individuality, the Supreme would also be made up of these three faculties — each functioning at their most perfect levels. Because He remains beyond the play of things in the physical realm, the power and sharpness of these inherent capabilities never decrease. His original qualities are neither lost nor diminished.

Before coming here from the soul world, we also had qualities similar to those of the Supreme but not to the same unlimited extent. If I identify myself totally with the physical body, the idea that God created human beings 'in His image' may have led me to believe that the human form is God's image. Perhaps that is how we created the medieval figure of an old white-bearded man sitting up in the heavens, controlling, rewarding and punishing as He deems fit. Whenever God is depicted in modern-day cartoons, it is as such. The paradox is that such a 'God' appears to have been created in our image, with both our best virtues and our worst defects - from the loftiest benevolence to the most almighty jealousy.

FORM

Anything that exists must have a form. Qualities indeed, are formless, but their source cannot be. For example, fragrance has no form but the flower does. Just as the sun has form but the light and warmth it radiates do not, God has a form, but the qualities radiating from Him do not. In other words, God is not love but the source of love; God is not truth but the source of truth, and so on.

9 *Genesis ch. 1, ver. 27*

As the soul is a point of light, of conscious energy, surrounded by an oval-shaped aura, the Supreme Soul is also. The only difference is in the degree and intensity of the qualities. Knowing His form, I can bring that image onto the screen of my mind and begin immediately to experience powers and qualities by associating them with that beautiful form. There is so much value in meditating on God's form and attributes. In all cultures and religions there is some special memorial or ritual in which light is always allied to what is holy or sacred. It's a reminder of the form of God as light. Candles, flames and other light sources have always held importance in religious practices.

The near-death experience, in which the conscious entity leaves the body usually due to some traumatic happening, lends meaning to this point. The individuals relate how they pass through a long tunnel at the end of which they perceive a light which is self-luminous and conscient. The light gives them a sense of relationship and warmth, possessed of non-judgmental love and compassion. The interesting thing about all these reports on near-death experiences is that, independent of their background — religious or even non-religious — their experience of this Being of light and love is identical.

REMEMBRANCE AS THE FORM OF LIGHT IN DIFFERENT RELIGIONS:

In the *Bhagavad Gita*, considered the main scripture of the Hindu religion, there is the phrase:

'If the effulgence of a thousand suns were to appear in the skies simultaneously, it might compare somewhat with the splendour of that great form'.[10]

This phrase comes at a point in the story in which Arjuna (who represents human beings) asks the Supreme how to *'see Your Divine form'.*[11] While the description may represent the awe and reverence of the devotees who wrote the scripture, the idea of God as light certainly comes through.

In the Old Testament Moses had a vision of God:

'And the angel of the Lord appeared unto him in a flame of fire out of the midst of a bush: and he looked, and, behold, the bush burned with fire, and the bush [was] not consumed. And Moses said, I will now turn aside, and see this great sight, why the bush is not burnt.

'And when the Lord saw that he turned aside to see, God called unto him out of the midst of the bush, and said, "Moses, Moses". And He said, "Here [am] I".'[12]

In the New Testament, the apostle John describes how Jesus Christ referred to God:

'This then is the message which we have heard of Him, and declare unto you, that God is light, and in Him is no darkness at all.'[13]

In the principal scripture of Islam, the *Koran*, there is the following

10 *Bhagavad Gita ch. 11, ver. 12*

11 *Bhagavad Gita ch. 11, ver. 3*

12 *Exodus ch.3 ver.2-4*

13 *John ch. 1 ver. 5*

GOD, LIGHT TO ALL

CHRISTIANITY,
THE ETERNAL LIGHT
REPRESENTING A LIVING
GOD

ATON, EGYPTIAN GOD
SHOWN AS A DISC OF
THE SUN

BIAIME, THE SUPREME OF
ABORIGINAL DREAMING,
REPRESENTS THE ENERGY
WHICH THAT BEING GIVES TO
ALL AROUND IT.

SHAMASH,
BABYLONIAN
SUN GOD

AHURA MAZDA,
THE WINGED DISC
OF ZOROASTER

INTI, SUPREME
GOD OF THE
INCAS

THE MENORAH
OF JUDAISM,
THE LIGHT THAT
REKINDLES
OTHER LIGHTS

reference:

'God is the light of the heavens and the earth; His light is as a niche in which is a lamp, and the lamp is in a glass. The glass is as though it were a glittering star . . .'[14]

FURTHER EXAMPLES

Many of the ancient religious practices involved some form of sun-worship. As the regulator of the change between day and night as well as the benevolent source of heat and light, the sun is the most visible model of God's more incognito role as a source of spiritual energy.

Here are some more examples.

- ✪ Surya, the sun-god is glorified in the Vedic hymns of India as all-seeing and all-knowing, similar attributes to the later Greek sun-god, Helios.

- ✪ The Egyptian sun-god Re (sometimes Ra) became the basis of a universal god, Aton, in the reign of Ikhnaton. The god was represented by a disc whose rays fell on all nobles and commoners alike.

- ✪ In the Sumerian epic of Gilgamesh the sun-god, Shamash, is shown as the constant supporter of the heroes.

- ✪ From its origin in Persia, the god of light, Mithra, brought to the Greeks by way of the Persian Wars, ended up as Sol Invictus (the unconquered sun) instituted by the Roman emperor, Aurelian, as the state cult in A.D.274. One of the most joyous of all Roman feasts was that of Sol Invictus on December 25th, eventually taken over by the Christians as Christ's birthday as so called paganism was absorbed.

- ✪ The Incas worshipped the sun-god, Inti – still the name of the Peruvian currency.

- ✪ The Aztec religion was centred around Huitzilopochtli, also a symbol of the sun.

- ✪ The North American Plains Indians typified the almost universal reverence of the sun in their famous sun-dance.

- ✪ In Japan, the sun-goddess, Amaterasu, was the supreme ruler of the world and deity of the imperial clan. Her symbol, the sun, continues to be represented on the Japanese flag.

- ✪ The Zoroastrians worship God as fire.

- ✪ Guru Nanak, the founder of the Sikh religion, called God *Ek Omkar,* the one Incorporeal Being.

THE OVAL-SHAPED IMAGE

All throughout India the most common representation of God is as an oval-shaped pillar which is set upright and worshipped by pouring milk and other oblations on it. They are called Shiva-lingums, representing the creative principle. The names of the temples where they are located attests to this: Somnath, the Lord of Nectar; Vishwanath, the Lord of the Universe; Mukteshwara, the Lord of Liberation.

---

14 *The Koran ch. XXIV para. 20*

After God had spoken to him, Abraham's grandson, Jacob, *'set up a pillar in the place where he talked to him, even a pillar of stone: and he poured a drink offering thereupon, and he poured oil thereon'*[15]

According to Islamic legend, when Adam left paradise, he came to a low hill upon which he saw a shining white oval stone. Around this stone he circled seven times, praising God. He then built the K'aaba. By the time of Abraham it needed to be rebuilt as a temple to honour the one God. The town of Mecca grew around this spot. This oval stone, later called *Sang-e-aswad* and now blackened by the kisses of millions, so they say, is the greatest object of pilgrimage in the whole of Islam.

A Buddhist sect in Japan focuses the mind on a small oval shape. They call it Karni, the peace-giver.

The fact that so many of our ancient traditions seem to be pointing to the same being of light is testimony to the commonality that binds humanity together as one race. We have all been worshipping and trying to discover the same God. There is only one God, and His form is light. If union between the soul and the Supreme Soul is to take place, it can only be possible if there is knowledge of that form.

NAME

Anything that has form also has a name. So too, God has a name. There are as many names for God as there are languages, and each name highlights one of God's specialities, but there is one name that perhaps describes God best.

When a human soul takes a body, it is the body that bears the name and not the soul. God's name is eternal and is based on attributes and functions. When God was talking to Moses, He said, *'And I appeared unto Abraham, unto Isaac, and unto Jacob, by the name of God Almighty, but by* **my**[16] *name, Jehovah, was I not known to them.'*[17]

The word *Jehovah* is probably related to the sanskrit word *Shiva*[18] which describes God quite accurately. It has three

Face to face,
the meeting place
in the mind's eye.
Heart to heart,
you fill my part
to the highest high.
Impressions for eternity, my Love.
Recorded for all history, my Love.
I couldn't think You'd come to me
so simply
and treat me to the sweetness of
Your words.
Mind to mind,
you clear the line
to your treasure store..
You and I, embraced in thought
forever more,
sealed to Truth eternally, my Love.
Living once again in Light, my Love.
I couldn't think You'd come to me
so simply
and treat me to the magic of Your words.

---

15 *Genesis ch. 35 ver. 14*

16 *The emphasis here is deliberate and not in the original.*

17 *Exodus ch. 6, ver. 3*

18 *Shiva is not to be confused with the figure of Hindu mythology who is called Shiva. That Shiva is also sometimes known as Shankar or Shiv-Shankar.*

meanings: benefactor, the seed of creation and point-source – and implies that there can be no other creator superior to that one. It describes the form as a point and the role as benefactor and the seed of humanity.

The word *Shiva* is the introduction to God, but in meditation another word is more applicable. The word is *Baba* or *Father* (literally *Father* or *Elder One*) which conveys the closeness and sweetness of the relationship I have with God. So the name *Shiva Baba* conveys God's role and my relationship with that One.

RESIDENCE

When we turn our minds to God, wherever we may be and from whichever culture, the first thing we normally do is to close our eyes in order to go beyond the world of people and objects. Intuitively we know that God exists beyond matter. If we ourselves are souls and not bodies, our real and eternal existence is on another plane. It's in that same dimension that God exists.

The home of the soul is a region of subtle, golden-red light, which can be visualised during meditation. It is from here that I come to take on my bodily forms. Just as my real home is the soul world, it is also the home of the Supreme Being. It doesn't mean that He/She is millions of light years away from me. I can reach that One in one thought, just as a dialled phone-call connects instantly. He/She is only one thought distant from me.

In this region of absolute stillness, silence and purity, God is able to remain perfectly stable, constant and unchanging, while the rest of the universe and the souls go through constant change.

ATTRIBUTES

On the basis of our similarities of form and abode, I learn from God of my own original attributes of peace, purity, love, truth, power, happiness and balance. By tuning my thoughts to that One, the influence begins to activate these original qualities in me.

God has often been described as the *Ocean of all Qualities* — limitless and constantly available. It's important not just to think of this being of light as the

PERSONAL EXPERIENCE

The further I went along the path, the more I began to comprehend some of the contradictions to which I had accustomed myself. The questions began: If God, the Supreme Power, is in each atom, or even within my heart, where then are His qualities of peace, love and wisdom? Someone once told me that there is a curtain of ignorance and illusion (maya) that separates me from the full realisation of the God within. Is this curtain of illusion, then, so powerful that it can cover God? In that case it would be God! If he were omnipresent, he would also be the curtain. If I am permeated by God, how could ignorance have come to me in the first place? Can ignorance affect God? If God is in me or all around, where can I direct my thoughts if I want to think of him? And so the questions went on ...

As the curtain of the consciousness 'I, the body' was being removed, I started having a notion of my true existence. I am not the physical body. At the time of death I leave it behind. As an eternal being I am involved in another dimension where there is neither time nor space. If I can exist on this more subtle plane, how is it possible for God to permeate the physical universe?

(E Phillips Fox, Motherhood (Detail) 1908 AGNSW)

In absolute terms, that One is the Supreme Mother whose love is totally accommodating

source of all positive attributes but also in terms of different relationships.

God's superiority lies in the depth, sharpness and continuity of His attributes. While human souls fluctuate between qualities such as peace and peacelessness, love and conflict, knowledge and ignorance, agony and ecstasy, God is ever-constant. He remains beyond the fields of change and relativity.

RELATIONSHIPS

To the extent to which I am able to make my own personal link with God, I develop in my personality aspects which are missing. Through relationships with other human beings I have been trying to fill the empty gaps in my emotional make-up. Now, I can complete what is missing, through loving contact with the Supreme Source of all attributes.

GOD AS MOTHER AND FATHER

In an overwhelming proportion of traditions God is a male figure. Just as the soul is neither masculine nor feminine, God has no gender. Therefore, as a soul, I can come close without any awe or difficulty caused by the gender of the body I am now occupying.

In absolute terms, that One is the Supreme Mother whose love is totally accommodating. No matter what has happened, how I am, good or bad, I experience unconditional acceptance. It's a love that empowers and cleanses. She is also the Supreme Father who offers protection and provides the inheritance of divine qualities. It's a question of just being an innocent child and claiming that inheritance – letting go of all the sorrow and pain which have been burdening the soul.

These are the first two relationships that have to be experimented with :

God as the mother and father. In the perfect personality of the Supreme there is the feminine principle of loving, giving and accepting. This is perfectly balanced with the masculine principle of power, authority and strength. He is She and She is He.

These parental relationships with God as Mother and Father are the foundation of my spiritual development. The concept of taking a new spiritual birth – of letting go of the past and developing a new consciousness – is a familiar one. It refers to becoming an innocent child again in the sense of purity, openness and wonderment.

The awareness of the self as a soul already changes my perspective enormously, but the consciousness of being a child of God and seeing others with that vision brings self-esteem, dignity, love and respect. Then all these things spill out in my connections with others. If I respect and value myself, I'll do the same for others.

Because God is a soul, neither old or young, male or female, and has the most perfect personality, there are so many different ways I can entertain myself in this highest and purest of all relationships.

BENEFITS OF OTHER RELATIONSHIPS

TEACHER	Discovery of wisdom and truth.
SUPREME GUIDE	Directions for each step on the spiritual path.
FRIEND	Conversation, support at any moment.
BELOVED	Sharing of intimacies, long-term support.
MANAGER	Readiness to execute instructions
CHILD	Giving of all I have.
HEALER	Correct diagnosis and cure of weaknesses.
BROKER	Wise investment for my future.

PURPOSE OF RELATIONSHIP WITH GOD

Raja Yoga means having a relationship with God. It is the only relationship that can transcend the span of a life-time which is the limit of human relationships. Being beyond time and distance, it's the only relationship which is continual. Even though I forget, it doesn't finish.

The essence of *yoga* or union is embodied in an idea that occurs in both Eastern and Western traditions – that God creates human beings in His own image. I allow my mind to start communicating with God so that it is cleansed and can fill itself with that pure, perfect love and start being a channel of that love into the world. Through contact and relationship with the Supreme Mind which has no barriers, limits or impurities, the quality of my mind changes. I am drawn away from limited and coloured perceptions to a state of purity and clarity in which there can be truth. I am able to change my personality traits through that influence so that my actions are motivated, not just by what I want, but by what is of benefit to the self and others.

Being created in God's image is a process which doesn't have anything to do with the creation of the body but with the re-energising of my original qualities though *yoga* with that One. It's the change from humanity to divinity.

THE PRESENCE OF GOD

I need to understand that God is a person (albeit the Supreme Person), like us, and not some diffused or impersonal energy. If I know God's form, location and attributes, I can direct my thoughts towards that One and immediately start experiencing the connection.

The sentiment expressed in the phrase, 'Lord, wherever I am, You are with me', indicates the closeness of the soul and God. It expresses the experience of the presence of God, in a similar way to two lovers who carry each other in their hearts. In this way God's presence is a spiritual experience that I can have wherever I am. It doesn't mean literally that the Supreme Being permeates everything. It's a feeling and not a fact.

The sun is the source of our physical necessities. It purifies the water, makes the plants grow to produce food and oxygen and provides a suitable range of temperatures for our life here. To give life it doesn't need to be present in every particle. Its effect in the form of light and heat is felt throughout the solar system.

In the same manner, for the effective practice of Raja Yoga meditation God is seen as a sun of perfect attributes, the source of spiritual qualities and powers and, as such, doesn't need to be present in everything. Even though His residence is the soul world, God can be with me since the sense of closeness is beyond physical dimensions.

One thought and I am in God's presence!

THE POWER OF GOD

The powers of God are often misunderstood. We think that, because God is almighty, He/She can do anything and everything and has direct influence on nature and on our lives. Birth and death, accidents and natural calamities are part of the interplay between human souls themselves and with matter directly. They are nothing to do with God.

The physical, chemical and biological laws of nature are automatic and do not require God's intervention. Our lives are really governed by the Law of *Karma*[19], or cause and effect. Happiness and sorrow are the automatic results of our *own* interactions. The good things and the bad are neither God's blessings nor the lack of them but a result of our own deeds.

In a state of spiritual frailty I instil many contradictions into my mind-set. On one hand I say that God is beyond my comprehension; yet, when something happens that I don't comprehend, I often take recourse to the phrase, 'It is God's will'.

But my heart asks, 'If God is the Ocean of Love, surely His will would be the manifestation of that love?' It is not His will to kill people, nor is it His

19 See chapter 4

power to bring them back to life. God doesn't make the grass grow and the wind blow nor does He bind the energy of the atoms together. He is not the dispenser of our roles. It is because we have misunderstood His powers that we seek His favour in our places of worship: 'Grant us this..., Give me that...', and so on. Though we flatter God to accede to our requests, when something goes wrong, He is blamed most solemnly with the phrase, 'It is the will of God'.

God cannot infringe the immutable laws which govern His interplay with souls and nature, nor grant favours to some and not to others. God will not remove my burdens, unless I make the efforts necessary. He/She is immune to both flattery and defamation.

God's greatness lies not in the ability to intervene in events whenever He/She chooses but in that He/She alone is the only one in the universe who upholds these laws perfectly and forever. The Supreme Soul uses His power for the benefit of the world — to transform it when it reaches extreme degradation. God's power is purely spiritual!

THE KNOWLEDGE OF GOD

God's knowledge is also spiritual. It is because of what He knows that He can be the Ocean of Love and Peace. Understanding this world does not necessarily mean to know the detailed movements of every single leaf or molecule. All that is required is to understand the conditions through which things pass.

The laws of nature automatically take care of the details of nature, as the law of cause and effect *(karma)* takes care of the details of human life. In order for Him to perform His task it is just not necessary for that One to know our every thought, our every secret.

God knows and accepts that everything that happens is part of an eternal drama that He did not create but in which He finds Himself the principal actor. He alone has the right to give knowledge regardless of human arguments.

If we knew what He/She does, then maybe we could get out of the mess we've succeeded in creating for ourselves.

THE ACTS OF GOD

God has a role to play in the drama of creation, just as we have. Though exactly what His role is and has been remains an area of hot debate, it's essential to see all possibilities in a logical and dispassionate manner so I can draw the best conclusions.

GOD, SOULS AND MATTER

The interplay of the basic components of our existence can be summed up in the following points.

✪ There are three distinct and eternal operative realities, each having its own powers and functions : God, souls, and matter (or nature). They are all separate, but work together to produce the scenes of creation.

✪ There are two fields of existence : the physical and the metaphysical. Both fields act, react and interact to produce all events in the drama of creation, of which we are all a part, including God.

✪ On the physical level there is the interaction between souls and matter which produces all phenomenal events.

✪ On the metaphysical level there is the interaction between souls and God, the remembering and forgetting of that One, which gives the interesting plots and by-plots to the movement of events that we call world history.

✪ God acts on human souls and they, in turn, act on matter, which simply accompanies the changes in the souls. When souls come into the process of entropy, matter simply follows.

✪ God neither created Himself, nor human souls nor matter.

As I more deeply understand the law of cause and effect, dealt with in the next chapter, I can see that it is impossible for God to have been the literal physical creator of this world and human beings.

GOD AS CREATOR

Reason tells me that spiritual and material energy in the form of souls and matter didn't just suddenly appear out of nothing. The First Law of Thermodynamics states that energy can't be either created or destroyed. Matter itself is a form of condensed energy. Souls are also conscious points of energy. Both are *uncreated and therefore eternal*.

The Second Law shows us that energy, when in use, moves from a potential state, in which energy is available, to a spent state in which it is no longer available.

Putting both laws together we have what appears to be a system in which the basic components have neither beginning nor end. They move towards a state of energy exhaustion (entropy). If time were linear and there were no external intervention, then over an unimaginably long period of time the universe would just fizzle out.

Fortunately for both the souls and the elements of matter, there is one supreme energy source which is external to the process of entropy and thereby retains its original potency. When things reach a certain stage of weakness and chaos, the Supreme Soul plays out His role of re-energising the souls. The recuperation to their original state, in turn, has a direct effect on matter. It also comes back to its own original state of perfection.

If, as has been shown above, God's presence, power and knowledge are purely spiritual, then creation has to be a spiritual act and not a physical one. Creation can be understood as the regeneration or reshaping of what is already there. He/She recharges the souls' spent spiritual energy.

The verse in the Bible — '*In the beginning was the Word and the Word was with God and the Word was God...*'[20] — indicates one of the Supreme Soul's basic qualities as the embodiment of knowledge. Through imparting clear and concise knowledge about the soul and its true relationship with that One, human beings are able to connect themselves once again with the source of spiritual power. Their transformation changes everything.

GOD AS SUSTAINER

Again I have to understand the difference between physical and spiritual sustenance. I may think that God is the sustainer in the sense that He gives us our goods, wealth, health, food, water, air and so on. If that were so, why should

(Vasily Kandinsky Various Actions (Detail) Solomon R. Guggenheim Museum)

God, souls, and matter (or nature).
They are all separate, but work together
to produce the scenes of creation.

He give more of these things to some and not to others? Why do poverty, starvation and disease exist if God is a sustainer and provider of all in the physical sense?

Whatever I do or do not possess I have earned for myself. It is not God who pays the wages. Whatever fruits I earn are the results of my own efforts. As a spiritual sustainer, He fills us with His power, virtues and knowledge to help us in our spiritual endeavour and does not put bread on our tables.

GOD AS DESTROYER

There are many allegories about a vengeful God, destroying whole armies who dared to stand in the way of His chosen ones. We have even gone to war, extolling the righteousness of our causes and counting on God's support. Somehow the heart rejects the idea of God as a destroyer of life. He/She is the destroyer of evil and the creator of virtue.

For example, there is the tale of the crossing of the Red Sea by the Israelites[21] and the subsequent destruction of their Egyptian slave masters. This tale appears in many cultures, only with different names, places and dates. On one side, there is the land of affliction and suffering (in this case, Egypt), and on the other side, the land of milk and honey, the promised land. In between, there is a seemingly impassable sea which, by the grace of God, suddenly opens up and the chosen ones cross. Behind them, their former captors are swallowed up as God closes the water on them. The story is obviously symbolic.

The chosen ones, the true followers of God, have their path made easier for them through His unswerving guidance. They leave suffering behind and make the journey to the other side — to a *promised* elevated world. The weaknesses, their former *captors*, try to follow but are exterminated completely with God's help.

SIMILARITIES AND DIFFERENCES BETWEEN THE SOUL AND GOD

There are so many differences between the souls and the Supreme Soul that it is not logical to consider the self as being equal to that One, neither in terms of function nor in terms of power. Yet, the union or *yoga* with God is based on similarities and not differences.

SIMILARITIES	DIFFERENCES
Same form and size.	Human souls lose their original attributes, owing to identification with the body; God never comes into the cycle of birth and rebirth.
Same eternal metaphysical power.	Human souls oscillate in terms of nature. God remains eternally stable.
Same original state: pure, full of virtues and spiritual power.	We forget who we are and where we are from; God retains knowledge of the whole process.

MEDITATION – A LINK OF LOVE

Through knowledge I create a link with God but, if it's only an intellectual connection, it will not remain stable. Through the understanding of the method of Raja Yoga I can build a bridge between myself and the Supreme but it's only with love that I can cross it. If there is no knowledge, there is no bridge. Having love alone leaves me on my side of the bridge, alone and unfulfilled.

Using the starting point of a deep appreciation of the method of meditation,

21 *Exodus ch. 14*

I can begin to develop the experience of pure love for the One who is the essence of all relationships: Mother, Father, Teacher, Friend, Guide and so on. Any relationship in which affection can exist is possible between the soul and the Supreme Soul.

Because of the subtle nature of meditation practice an intellectual approach is inadequate. Both the soul and God are incorporeal. It's only love that can propel me towards that One and keep me connected in a concentrated way. In Raja Yoga I meditate not just on myself but also on the nature and qualities of the Supreme Soul. The main purpose of meditation is to be able to communicate with God in order to be able to experience a relationship with Him.

Perhaps I have already had the experience of deep love for God without any conscious information. In this case, meditating on or remembering God with love comes easily. For others love grows on the basis of deepening experiences.

THERE ARE FOUR STEPS IN MEDITATION PRACTICE.

✪

Detach the self from negative, wasteful and mundane thinking

✪

Create pure or elevated thoughts about my original state and about my original home

✪

Visualise myself as a point of conscious light energy directly in front of God in His radiant form of light

✪

Open myself to receiving God's love

In human terms, there might be a spontaneous feeling of love for someone and, on another level, I might recognise the need for that person in my life and so a relationship grows. It's built on the basis of that need. Unfortunately, because of our limitations, there always seems to be a price to pay. If I take from another in some way, at some point, even in the most altruistic of relationships, there will be a price to pay. Basically this happens because every human being has a need. Each one of us looks towards others to be able to fulfil that need.

The idea of God as the absolute source is very appealing. In meditation there is the awareness that I am turning to the source of love who will never expect anything in return. He/She is the only soul who has no need!

TRANSMITTER AND RECEIVER

The analogy of a radio transmitter and receiver helps me understand the nature of meditation. Whatever frequency I tune the set to, the transmissions are received accordingly. If my mind is tuned to the world of human beings, then I get those types of messages. If I make the effort to take my consciousness above all this, then I am able to start receiving from the

Supreme Soul. The experiences are not just of filling the self but of self–transformation.

Whether my relationship with God begins out of pure love or the love gradually develops, the most powerful discovery is that it's on the basis of this relationship that I can actually start changing myself. It's the same as in human relationships. The more intimate the relationship, the greater the influence.

The interactive process of mind, intellect and *sanskars* or, in other words, thought, decision, action, imprint and stimulus for further thought, needs an infusion of power so that it can stop its negative spinning. Whether there is an addiction to substances or situations, or to subtle addictions such as anger, attachment or greed, the only way to break out of either is by injecting strength into the process.

Knowing myself is one thing; recognising my own weaknesses and strengths is another thing. The negativity in the world outside stimulates my own defects even though I know that somewhere inside me are the jewels of virtues that seem to be hidden very deep. Learning to access the beauty of the self and my original quality is definitely the first step.

Still, I need power to be able to break free from the difficult trap that I have got myself into. On my own I am not able to generate that power. If I turn to another human being, it becomes another trap in itself. One addict trying to support another is not the most effective way to generate the power to transform.

The alternative is to turn to the source of spiritual power — God, the Supreme Soul. Coming to the realisation that I need help from the Supreme isn't a sign of weakness but of wisdom and recognition.

It is soul-consciousness that creates the foundation for me to have this understanding of the one from whom to take strength. Besides being the source of love, truth and beauty, the Supreme Being is also the source of power and light. Through connection with that One all these qualities become available. All I have to do is to make that link and it all starts flooding in.

The only effort I make is to tune my consciousness. That is my responsibility. If I let myself spin around in circles here and there, even though the help may be pouring in, I won't know how to take it. I'll even be unaware of its availability.

It's necessary to experiment with depth and love in each relationship, and not just to think of the Supreme Being as a point of light.

The benefits of meditation are summed up as follows:

✪ transformation of the negative personality traits
✪ obtaining power for self-control (eg. in a situation of anger or irritation, the soul is able to overcome its negative tendencies)
✪ improvement of the vision one has of the self and others
✪ inner emotional fulfilment through each of the relationships
✪ replacement of lost or spent spiritual and mental energy.

It's when I discover the art of silence and how to still my mind that I realise how much mischief and wildness were there previously. In those first moments of indescribable peace in meditation all the postponement of effort to improve spiritually is seen for what it is – just needless loss.

The subject of God takes on a new meaning, if only for the reason that in that One I can find the source of power and love to overcome the consequences of my weakened state in which negativity has proliferated in an uncontrolled manner.

I need to know the self and be still to be able to make the mental connection or union with the Supreme Soul. Equally, I need to have the details about who, what, and why God is, so that the contact is not just theoretical but so real that it can blossom into a meaningful relationship. Raja Yoga in its deepest sense is just that: learning to develop a relationship with God.

SUMMARY
- The deepest meaning of Raja Yoga meditation is to connect the individual soul with God, the Supreme Soul.
- To do this I have to have a clear idea of how and where to connect up, i.e. the form, name, residence and attributes.
- The soul and the Supreme Soul have the same form: an infinitesimal starlike point of conscious energy surrounded by an oval aura.
- The home of the soul and of God is the same one — the soul world.
- The best name to describe God is *Shiva* — the incorporeal benefactor, seed of creation.
- God is the perfect mind and intellect. His *sanskars* are of unlimited love, peace, happiness, truth, purity and balance. Human souls have these attributes in their original state but God is unchanging. He is the constant ocean of all positive qualities.
- God is the essence of all relationships: Mother, Father, Teacher, Guide, Friend and so on.
- God's presence, powers and knowledge are spiritual and not physical.
- God's three acts of creation, sustenance and destruction are all spiritual.
- He/She creates or renews the historical process through recharging and imparting knowledge to human souls. He/She sustains spirituality through the strength of that knowledge and power. He/She destroys negative tendencies in human souls.
- Meditation means relationship with God through remembering His qualities and acting according to them.

Karma teaches me that I am the creator of my own little world. I also am the creator of the environment immediately around me. On a greater level I am a co-creator together with God of the world of tomorrow.

(Marc Chagall Autour d'elle, Musee National d'Art Moderne Florence)

Chapter 4

Karma and Yoga

The steps are the most important part of any journey. The process of getting there is every bit as important as arriving. The steps of my journey towards higher consciousness are what I actually do and not just think or speak. Intellectualising about elevated actions is fine if I have the determination to carry them out. I need to know how to translate what I learn, through information, into a practical reality.

While I am unaware of my true identity, it isn't possible to discover exactly how every action that is performed leaves an impact or impression in the form of a sanskar within myself. Some of these imprints have a beneficial effect and others not.

By understanding the relationship between my state of consciousness and my day-to-day activities, I can start to transform my life. The seeds of actions are in my state of consciousness. The fruits are in the situations I create for myself. By learning about the tandem nature of what happens around me and what happens within me, I can start to take my destiny into my own hands and employ the instruments of change.

I need also to comprehend the part that God plays in human affairs. I should neither try to put the blame on a devil figurehead for the vices that have assailed human values and activities nor unreasonably expect the Supreme Being to put things right without any effort on my part. Both attitudes put real change beyond my grasp and set me up for alternating between despair, on one extreme of the spectrum, to pleading for help, on the other.

If there is only one process to which all beings and things are tied, then it affects us all without exception. We know there are physical, biological and chemical laws which are exact and immutable. For example, hydrogen always reacts with oxygen to form the water molecule under given circumstances. Just as these laws govern the behaviour of physical particles there are laws that govern the behaviour of the metaphysical entities called souls.

As I start to move forward on the spiritual path, it becomes increasingly important to understand and take on board the process that some have referred to as the Law of Karma. Spirituality also possesses systematic laws.

In this chapter we will explore the following:
- ✪ a clear definition of the Law of *Karma*
- ✪ the part that God plays in human events
- ✪ evidences of the karmic process and rebirth
- ✪ *Karma Yoga* in actions and relationships
- ✪ how to strengthen the conscience and change deeply ingrained habits
- ✪ four different types of karma: for the self, for or with others, for leisure and for the spiritual benefit of others.

DEFINITION OF KARMA

The word *karma* has been passed on to the West, coloured by some negative connotations. In common usage it is almost always related to suffering. In fact, it simply means action. When we refer to the Law of *Karma* it definitely denotes action and its result or, simply, cause and effect.

It is the metaphysical equivalent of Newton's First Law — every action has an equal and opposite reaction.

THE ABSOLUTENESS OF THE LAW OF KARMA

The word *absolute* can be used to refer to the Law of *Karma*. I cannot play around with it. Human laws can be adjusted, manipulated and even side-tracked, but with the Law of *Karma* it is just not possible.

Whatever I put out is going to come back to me; I am going to reap the fruit of whatever I sow. On the physical level there is no time gap between the action and its reaction. I throw a ball in the air and it falls back immediately with the same force. With the Law of *Karma*, however, there can be a delay between the sowing and the reaping. The seeds of certain actions bring instantaneous results. Others can take years or even lifetimes to come to fruit.

If I eat too much chocolate, I will see the repercussions or karmic effect of that greed within a space of thirty minutes. Many actions, however, have their return much later, creating consternation, as I try to work out what's going on.

I see the effects of actions and do not realise that the cause may have actually been in a previous life. There is a total connection between the cause and the effect.

On a larger scale I can analyse a natural calamity such as an enormous storm that blows off roofs, overturns cars, uproots trees and even kills people. The physical causes may be the coming together of high and low atmospheric pressure systems. At the time, it's no use saying that it's an act of God. At the same time, it's not usual to think that such a problem could have its roots in a process of environmental imbalance initiated by human beings hundreds of years ago.

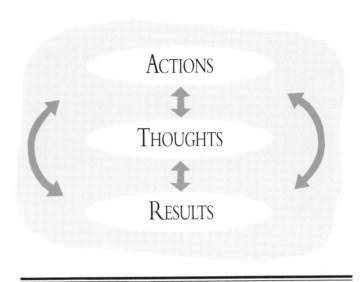

CAUSE AND EFFECT

On a personal level I can say that there is nothing that happens to me for which I am not responsible. Whether I remember what I did to make it happen or whether I realise it or choose to ignore it, I am ultimately responsible.

I can start experimenting with this idea instantly. If I want to change results, I have to change my thoughts and actions. For example, if I have good thoughts for others, those thoughts will reach them. Whatever their feelings may have been towards me, if I have good wishes towards them, sooner or later, their feelings will start to change towards me and the relationship will improve.

The quality of thoughts determines my personal level of happiness. Our mental natures are the result of everything we have thought; they are ordered by our thoughts, formed by our thoughts. The first words of the Buddha in the *Dhammapada* underline this deep truth: '*If a man speaks or acts with an evil thought, sorrow will follow him as the cart goes after the ox*'.

MOTIVE DETERMINES RESULT

It's not so much the act that determines the return but the quality of intention behind it. In the simple task of brushing the teeth the intention can be varied.

- ✪ I need to clean them well; I don't want cavities. (care)
- ✪ What terrible teeth! What am I going to do? (anxiety)
- ✪ I have the most splendid teeth in the world! (vanity)

Each of these attitudes will lead to a different result.

This becomes even more obvious when analysing the difference in guilt between someone who accidentally kills another while cleaning a gun and another who plans for months to commit the murder. The act of taking away a life is the same but the return depends on the intention.

UNDERSTANDING THE LAW OF KARMA

Picture a person from London or Sydney who goes to New York for the first time and parks his rented car on the wrong side of the road. He'll get a ticket and have to pay a fine because parking and driving laws are different in both countries. He cannot simply plead ignorance. It should have been his responsibility, if driving, to find out the laws of the land and he did not bother.

In ignorance, we have done many things against the universal and divine laws. We cannot just say 'I didn't know'. Above a certain age it is our responsibility to know.

If we look at the state of the world now, there may be a few sparks of light but, generally, there is a great amount of darkness. That gives us an indication of the sorts of *karmas* we have been performing to have produced our situations.

The understanding of the karmic process is fundamental, if I want to:

✪ reduce the weight of the past

✪ eliminate any type of suffering

✪ modify the course of my life

✪ start to experience a positive return from my spiritual efforts

✪ understand all the whys which surround my daily life

QUESTIONS THAT LEAD TO TENSIONS

Why am I here? Why is she happy and I am not? Why did he do that to me? I've never seen him in my life. Why does that one have easy success in life and the other, however much he tries, can't get anything together? Why was that one born blind and without arms and the other healthy? Why does she suffer so much? She is so sweet and everyone treats her so badly. Why did that child die so horribly? She was so innocent. Why did I get married to such a person?

Why? What? For what reason? How? These inner questions tear at the fabric of the consciousness. Even so, they all have only one answer: *karma*. I don't need to go into minute details of each situation. If I see that nothing can happen without having had a just cause in my past or in that of others, life becomes much easier to face, with responsibility and courage.

BEING REALISTIC

The fact that the past irrevocably creates the present may seem pessimistic. In fact, it is the pathway to real freedom. It makes me accept that the responsibility for whatever has happened to me up to this moment, cannot be attributed to any another person, ancestors, the government or even God. It is mine and mine only. Equally, what my future holds depends on me. Rather, whatever I choose to do at this moment is already creating my destiny for tomorrow.

I shouldn't forget that the only real time I have for creating my future is the present, now. *Karma* teaches me that I am the creator of my own little world. I also am the creator of the environment immediately around me. On a greater level I am a co-creator together with God of the world of tomorrow.

That I can create the future of my choice — of love, peace and happiness — can appear as unreasonable optimism. It's just being realistic. What I create is what is going to happen. If I choose to exchange love and peace in my interactions with others, I create relationships based on those qualities.

THE PART THAT GOD PLAYS

The Law of *Karma* is part of the whole understanding of truth and justice. God is remembered as being the one who is the truth but also as the one who is just. God explains the Law of *Karma* so that I can understand what is right and what is just.

In *Brewer's Dictionary of Phrase and Fable* there is the following definition of *act of God:* 'The loss resulting from the action of forces uncontrollable by man is said to be due to an act of God and therefore has no legal recourse.'
The idea of God as the Punisher does not fit in with a God of love, mercy and compassion.

One may ask where God is at the time of disaster or extreme peacelessness. I have to understand that God's role is to bestow peace. In fact, it is the denial, rejection or avoidance of that One's existence that leads to brutality and violence on individual or collective levels. Human beings have the power to create. We have created the present situation of a world of immense pain and suffering on personal, community and international levels. My heart or conscience cannot say that God is responsible for that.

What happens in both our personal world and the world at large is the direct result of our actions. In ignorance we separated ourselves from God's influence and, as a result, negativity has become as strong and manifest as it has.

God's role within all of this at the present time is one of direct intervention. When there is just too much suffering and confusion, God's role is not to take a magic wand and - abracadabra! - the world changes. There are universal laws which He comes to teach so that we can start applying them. We knew them but forgot them.

EVIDENCES OF THE KARMIC PROCESS

The moment, place, social condition, type and sex of body and family of birth are determined by the individual soul itself. It's not a conscious act but the accumulated effect of the actions of the previous life or lives. There is no divine lottery that distributes roles, bodies, wealth or suffering in a random way. There is no divine power that says: 'This one will be born in the gutters of Calcutta and that one will go to the British royal family.' From this unlimited point of view, justice exists. Everything that happens in anyone's life is the fruit of his or her own recent or remote past.

The apparent social injustices, inept governments, needless bloodshed, physical, emotional or psychic pain are the consequences, on a personal or collective level, of the thoughts, words or actions of this or other lives. Conditions that exist for the positive development of society or the individual are also rewards from the past.

At first sight it seems that there is nothing one can do except surrender meekly and wait to receive these returns. This would be to understand only half of the karmic process. One still has the freedom to change one's direction and build the best future possible. If I look at my actions on a superficial level only, I won't understand anything. The true causes of my emotional or spiritual state are in the situations I created in the past.

KARMIC ACCOUNTS

There is an important corollary to the Law of *Karma*. We are not only individuals acting alone. We act in this extraordinary play of existence with other actors. During the process and according to the interaction with others, we create accounts of debit or credit that become the basis of our connections with others.

The reasons for which a specific relationship goes well or not are in the so called karmic account that I have accumulated with the other person. The beings that play the parts of parents, husbands, wives, children, friends, colleagues and acquaintances form a network for the giving and receiving of happiness and sorrow from this account established in the past or being created in the present. The strongest relationships that I have now were established previously. We knew each other in other lives and possibly in other connections. The son returns now as the husband, the friend of some births ago comes back as the brother and so on. This is why there is the hope that, after a brief separation at physical death, we can meet again with the loved ones who have passed on.

As long as the account exists, the interchange of actions together continues. When there is nothing more to give or receive, the paths separate by death, divorce or simply by the loss of contact. How many friends to whom eternal closeness was sworn in school days does one still have?

Not only the whys and wherefores of kinship and connections are easily understood by the karmic process but also our own inner natures. As was mentioned, everything that an individual does or produces is registered in the self as a *sanskar*. *Sanskars*, therefore, are not only the basis of the karmic accounts but also of our talents, personalities and propensities.

Mozart, at four years of age, wrote minuets, a concerto for piano and a sonata. These compositions were not only technically accurate but extremely difficult. At seven, he wrote a complete opera! Where could he have learned to play so well? It's obvious that such musical mastery at such a young age was not a genetic inheritance. He must have developed his talents previously.

A more common example is the following: A child is born into a family where, from the beginning, all efforts are undertaken to prepare him to be a doctor, according to family tradition. However, from an early age, the child shows strong tendencies to be an artist, starts to play around with colours and the talent again manifests itself. This demonstrates that the traits the soul carries internally from previous experiences will take it in a specific direction despite attempts to the contrary.

REBIRTH

Over half the world's inhabitants accept rebirth as a fact of life. Hindus, Buddhists, Taoists and others all adhere to a firm belief in this basic truth.

Henry Ford: 'Genius is experience. Some think that it's a gift or talent, but it is the fruit of long experience of many lives. Some are older souls than others and so know more…I would like to communicate with others the calmness that a more extensive vision of life gives us.'

They accept the Law of *Karma* as the *modus operandi* of human life on the planet.

In the sacred Hindu book, the *Bhagavad Gita (The Song of God)*, it is said:
'For the soul there is never birth nor death. Neither once existing will it cease to exist. It is non-born, eternal, always existent, immortal and primordial. It does not die when the body dies.' (ch.2:20).' Just as a person dresses with new clothes, dispensing with the old ones, in a similar way the soul accepts the new material bodies, dispensing with the old and useless ones.' (ch.2:22)

The teachings of the Buddha in the *Dhammapada* say:
'Better than the life of a hundred years of a man who does not perceive the immortal state is the short life of one day of a man who feels the immortal state. That one, I would call a true master, who knows the mystery of the death and rebirth of all beings, who is happy with himself and illuminated, and who is free from all attachments.'

In the *Koran* (the sacred book of Islam) there is the following verse:
'The person of a man is only a mask that the soul uses for a season. It lasts its correct

time and is left, and another is used in its place... I will tell you a truth: That the spirits which now have an affinity will have kinship, though all of them meet in new persons and names.'

The father of mass-production and one of the geniuses of the twentieth century, Henry Ford, said in an interview:

'I adopted the theory of reincarnation when I was 26... Religion didn't give me the answers... Even work didn't give me complete satisfaction. Work is futile if we can't use the experiences we gather in one life in the next. When I discovered reincarnation, it was as if I had found a universal plan. I realised that there was time to work with my ideas...

Genius is experience. Some think that it's a gift or talent, but it is the fruit of long experience of many lives. Some are older souls than others and so know more... I would like to communicate with others the calmness that a more extensive vision of life gives us.'

The psychologist Carl Jung wrote in his book *Memories, Dreams and Reflections:*

'My life, as I lived it, seemed to me many times like a story without beginning or end. I had the impression that I was a historic fragment, an extract from which the text before and after was missing. I imagined that I could have lived in past centuries and come across questions which I couldn't answer so that I had to be born again, as I had not fulfilled the task given me. When I die, my deeds will accompany me. That's how I imagine it to be. I will take with me all that I've done. Meanwhile, it's important to ensure that I don't reach the end empty-handed.'

Seeing the process of human existence on a personal level stretching back into the past and continuing on into the future definitely gives back a great degree of security to the soul. Affinities and aversions are understood. The feelings of having met someone before or passed by a specific place are so common that the idea of cosmic randomness just cannot remain. If there is such order in the minute details of cells and atoms, why cannot such order exist to determine relationships, stretching over a long period of time?

In the impossibility of complying with all karmic obligations in one life, we have to take a new body to guarantee that all beneficial and negative actions receive their due return.

It's not surprising that a great part of humanity believes in or at least has some notion of rebirth or reincarnation. Without mentioning such taboo words, modern-day Christians speak about the concept of resurrection that at least contains the principal aspect of the Law of *Karma* - that one receives the return for one's acts.

After all, we are spiritual beings and have all passed through the same process of being born, living, leaving the body at death and being reborn again in another body. As a spiritual being, with the same mind, intellect and personality that I have now, I have been in other bodies, have known other places and situations and have been involved in other relationships. To sum up: I am the same person I've always been!

LONG-TERM VISION

Since the soul is not its current personality, sex, religion or age and it has played so many different roles in the past, the future also promises great variety.

Let's say that a soul has the present role of being a white male, ugly and chauvinistic, and yet, in the previous life, was in the body of a black, beautiful and kind female. If he had this vision, how could he now sustain his chauvinism? It's like an immense game of role and costume changes involving the same actors.

If one knew that there was the possibility of being reborn in a body of the opposite sex in a completely different culture or society, one would, by necessity, have to inculcate the qualities of tolerance and respect. One would appreciate other cultures and learn one's lessons without internal blocks.

DEFINITION OF KARMA YOGA

To be a *raja yogi* means to be a ruler of the self. It's not just a question of learning to discipline the physical senses but, more importantly, of redirecting the energy of the mind, emotions and the personality in a positive and constructive way.

Raja Yoga can also be called *Karma Yoga*. It means to perform action while having a mental connection with the Supreme Being or to have a meditative consciousness while walking, talking, sitting on a bus, driving a car or working, in fact, doing anything.

Meditation is specifically related to the use of the mind and intellect. Even so, just as we can remember other things and people while involved in some activity, we can keep our minds on the Supreme Being and churn different aspects of spiritual knowledge.

The *yoga* is reflected through the *karma* that I do. Whatever work I do can now carry a different quality. Work itself, far from being just a means of survival, becomes the basis of real transformation. It was through action that the soul came down from its original state. It is through action that it can return to its previous glory. It's not just action for its own sake or for the self but action becomes the means through which I can share the experience I have in meditation.

My meditation isn't a secret process but a very visible one. I can see the results of *yoga* through my *karma*. If my actions are still aggressive or motivated by greed, this certainly serves as an internal check for what's happening with my meditation. If there is the experience of a link, then God's peace, light, love and purity are going to manifest themselves through my actions.

ACTIONS AND RELATIONSHIPS

We develop relationships with each other, not just through thinking, but through contact and interaction. The thought may be the starting point but, the very moment I move towards the other person through a telephone call or a visit, the process of giving and taking is initiated. The bond between a mother and child grows according to the physical, emotional and spiritual sustenance she gives it.

This occurs in any relationship. Two people come together and the actions they perform for and with each other reinforce the bond between them. The give and take can be of happiness or sorrow and all shades in between. A relationship can't exist without *karma* or interaction.

The same applies in my relationship with the Supreme Soul. Actions that are just for my own sense-gratification or for the development or sustenance of a relationship with another human being are called *karmas*. Actions performed out of love for or obedience to God are called *karma yoga*. Certainly there is no question of doing anything for God. He doesn't need or want anything.

A considerate parent would want his/her child's life, character and qualities to be most elevated. He/she would try to give directions to the child with that in mind. If the child acts accordingly, the bond becomes more meaningful. In the same way, to the extent that I follow God's instructions out of love, my relationship grows and my experience of *yoga* deepens.

There is also the idea that to serve one's neighbour is to serve God but what type of service? It depends on the motivation. If I do things for another to gain respect or admiration from them, it cannot be called service of God. If I genuinely see the other as my brother and share the fortune I've received from God with that individual, that pure and selfless act will bring me closer to God.

When we consider *yoga* in its practical form, it has nothing to do with leaving your work or family and seeking a cave in the mountains. *Karma yoga* means to live in the world but to maintain the link of *yoga* so that it transforms one's life and one's life can help to transform the world.

RIGHT OR WRONG?

The expression, *right and wrong,* can have many different interpretations in terms of history, culture, race, age and so on. But there's a very basic and simple touchstone that one can use that overrides all these other factors. If I first stabilise myself in the awareness of 'I, the Soul', separate from the body, whatever action I perform is going to be a positive action and right. If I allow this consciousness to slip and any of the other temporary or false masks and identities are adopted, that is, if I start to think of myself as an American or an Indian, as a man or a woman, then the action will inevitably be coloured by anger, greed, ego or attachment, even if only slightly. If I act in a limited consciousness, there will be an influence of negativity. In the eternal consciousness of who I am, the action will be pure.

Another very simple guideline to decide if an action is right or wrong is that, if it causes some sort of pain or sorrow, then probably it is influenced by some form of negativity. If it gives happiness to the spirit, then it probably is a pure action.

Both guidelines must work together as the second one can be confusing. Others may accuse me of causing them sorrow but it could well be that their own attachment is making them suffer, rather than anything I have done.

That is why the first criterion must always be applied. If an action is performed in my eternal consciousness, then not only will it bring benefit to me, but it will give happiness. The effect of pure *karma* is to bring myself and others around me closer to God. An action based on limited consciousness, which, relatively speaking, can be called impure, takes me and others away from God.

> *If I use my time well,*
> *I gain time.*
> •
> *If I use my energy well,*
> *I gain energy.*
> •
> *If I use my wealth well,*
> *I gain wealth.*
> •
> *In this way I find leisure*
> *in everything I do.*

STRENGTHENING THE CONSCIENCE

I can also experiment with the Law of *Karma* on the level of the inner process of the self. Within us there is a brake called *conscience* that somehow has ceased to function. In today's fast-paced world of thought-action, thought-action, there seems no pause in between to question the correctness of what is happening. Usually we do not give ourselves that space of allowing the conscience to do its task. We just move quickly from thought into action.

The role of God is to awaken the conscience. My task is to allow my conscience to be cleansed and refined through meditation so that it can start working as the filter that it is supposed to be. Deep down inside perhaps I recognise that a particular thought is not right or beneficial and yet, owing to the influence of company or my own desires, I ignore the voice of conscience and allow that thought to come into action. The continuance of such a process over a long period of time has quietened the voice of the conscience to the extent that it has stopped speaking altogether.

If a good friend sees that I am about to head in the wrong direction, he will try his best to warn me once, twice or even three times. If I do not heed his advice, he will give up and remain silent. We must learn not only to make the conscience a good friend but to pay attention to it so that it can gain back its original strength. In the constant flow of thought-action, thought-action, by not allowing the conscience to step in between, the quality of the *karma* has lost its high standard. The deterioration of the quality of *karma* is such that one only has to pick up a newspaper and see how much bad news there is about human *karma*.

Even after realising the difference between right and wrong, to be able to pull myself out of my own karmic trap of negative vicious cycles and both substance and emotional addictions, I need power. That is the ultimate purpose of meditation. In meditation, through the link with the Supreme Being, my conscience awakens and starts to become clearer so that I can see the difference, in terms of my life, between right and wrong. Also, I receive power to be able to make the right choices and to follow those through in my life. The quality of my *karma* changes as a result. The conscience is the voice of the original state of the soul. When awakened, those original qualities of peace, love, purity and power arise and assume control of the self. The very quality of my personality begins to change and develop in a positive direction. Just by being focused in the consciousness of being a soul and allowing my conscience to guide my life means that I am moving towards my destination with clarity and speed.

CHANGING DEEPLY INGRAINED HABITS

The amount of energy and willpower required to change one habit can be enormous. Those who have tried to give up smoking or to keep to a diet that necessitates less food intake can attest to this. But what about the personality traits formed over a long period of time or even over a period of births? The power required for this has to be deep and lasting.

The evidence of deeply ingrained character traits from the moment of birth is, in fact, convincing testimonial to continuity and the idea of previous existences.

To be able to change characteristics that one has been born with is generally considered as impossible as it is for a leopard to change its spots. Through *Raja Yoga* meditation I can observe deep personality changes taking place in a very positive way. *Raja Yoga* is a method of working directly on the soul itself. It empowers the intellect so as to give right direction to the decisions and actions. The quality of *karma* changes, which, in turn, is reflected in the *sanskars,* the repository of all habits and personality traits. From these purified *sanskars* elevated thoughts arise in a very natural, automatic way. This aspect of self-transformation is one of the main reasons for which I need to sit in meditation and practise stabilising my mind in the remembrance of God.

PRACTICAL EFFECTS OF *KARMA YOGA*

Karma yoga functions in two ways:
- ✪ by filling the self with power, the transformation of action is possible. This in turn brings about change in my *sanskars.*
- ✪ by drawing on the qualities of the Supreme Being my *sankars* change.

It's necessary to experiment with this to discover its validity. On one level, whatever I have done, I have to receive the return for that but, on another level, just simply pure love for God is the factor that purifies, cleanses and forgives. Whatever my past *karma* may have been, the fire of God's love is able to resolve it and remove its impact from within the soul itself, in terms of negative personality traits and also in terms of karmic effects in physical situations. Thus it can be seen why *yoga* or the union of love with God is so crucial.

FOUR TYPES OF KARMA

If one looks at the whole pattern of human life, there are four areas of *karma* which have to be improved:

- *Karma* that I perform for myself, for my own sustenance and upkeep.
- *Karma* that I perform with or for others in terms of relationships.
- *Karma* that I perform, not out of need or necessity, but for leisure.
- *Karma* that I perform as service of others.

KARMA THAT I PERFORM FOR MYSELF

If I, the soul, am the master of my body, then I have to look after its upkeep. The consciousness with which I feed and take care of the body has to be such that my actions don't bring me into further attachment to it. They have to be of such quality that they bring me closer to God and help to diminish my bodily ego or the pull towards physical desires. I have to work, cook, feed and wash the body but these activities can be done in such a way that they bring me closer to my destination of perfection, of freedom and of liberation.

KARMA WITH OR FOR OTHERS

There is specific energy that drives all relationships — that of credit and debit, give and take. These are the so called karmic accounts that have been created in the past and which now determine the quality and quantity of all our interactions and their results, in terms of joy or sorrow, in all our relationships.

It's not necessary to find out exactly what the karmic root cause of a problem in a relationship may have been. A very simple guideline to improve the quality of our interactions is:

Rather than take, let me give, so there won't be any further debts. Whether it is colleagues at work, family relationships or friends, let me see if there is a way in which I can fulfil my responsibility with integrity and honesty. If I am not doing that, if I am moving away from my responsibilities, I am adding to my karmic burden. In what way can I give or serve, so that there is no longer conflict, tension and struggle but just great sweetness and respect?

KARMA THAT I PERFORM FOR LEISURE

When someone says they don't have time for meditation or for their spiritual development, it generally reflects an unwillingness to face the self rather an actual lack of time. The fact that average T.V. viewing time in many countries runs to more than 15 hours a week tells its own story.

To the extent that I value my time, I value my life and make myself valuable. Valuing my time, energy and money is very much a part of the whole karmic story of give and take: what they are used for, how well they are used, whether they are abused and so on. Difficulties with time, one's own bodily energy and finances are the fruits of past indifference or abuse of these things. The world financial crisis is the karmic sum total of all such individual difficulties. Am I using all that I have in a worthwhile way? Am I just squandering it or am I using it for benefit for myself and for others? These questions, answered correctly, often spell the difference between success and failure.

KARMA THAT I PERFORM AS SPIRITUAL SERVICE OF OTHERS

Service of others can be seen on a very gross level as physical charity but the real service is to uplift the souls of others by inspiring them to reclaim their state of self-respect.

There is the old dictum that if I give others bread, I feed them for a day. If I teach them how to bake bread, I feed them for life.

In a spiritual way this refers to being able to show others the understanding of *karma* and how it works so that they can make efforts to transform their karmic situation. The ultimate, pure *karma* is to bring others closer to God.

SUMMARY

- ✪ Any flow of energy — thoughts, words or actions — is a *karma* which leaves its impression *(sanskar)* and has its return — good or bad.
- ✪ The soul is not immune to any action it performs.
- ✪ Positive *karma* is that which is in favour of the original state of the self or of others.
- ✪ Negative *karma* is that which is against the original state of the self or of others.
- ✪ The soul's purpose of taking a human body and coming here on to this world stage was in order to perform *karma*. It is to experience action and interaction and their repercussions.
- ✪ There isn't a single moment of our life here in which we are not influenced by or engaged in *karma*.
- ✪ Punishment and reward do not come from some superior being, a twist of divine providence, destiny or luck but are simply the effects of thoughts, words and actions created in the past. The individual either rewards or punishes himself.
- ✪ The past creates the present, which in turn produces the future; it has always been that way.
- ✪ I am not the victim of my past.
- ✪ It is to no purpose to cry over the past. I have to transform sorrow into learning. If I plant seeds of lamentation, the fruits will also be of that. If I sow joy, I reap joy.

- I am 100% responsible for my current situation, whatever it may be. I have definitely created it.
- I can change my present in such a way as to eliminate the burden created in the past.
- I am the architect of my own destiny. Fate, or destiny, is just the effect of my own acts.

Epilogue

Tying it all together

No matter how elevated the aim or how deep the philosophy, the bottom line of spirituality will always be how much I can translate into my practical life. The gap that separates ideal and practice touches all of us to a greater or lesser extent and spells the difference between satisfaction and frustration. Personal happiness is related to how well I align what I can believe to be true with my actions. If ideals provide the motivating factor which fuels my journey towards a higher consciousness, then practice is the methodology which burns it and takes me forward.

GOING BACK TO SCHOOL

If I so choose, life can be a constant battle from morning to evening, seven days a week. The road forward flashes by quickly. The years register their lines in my face, hands and heart as I try to make an increasing number of ends meet. The constant to and fro between family and work whittles away at my ideals, as I surrender to the prospects of a hard life and a not too comfortable retirement. If I let it, life can also itself become the source of my tensions as I continually seek scapegoats upon whom to heap blame. It is as if the path is strewn with boulders blocking my way. Instead of stepping around or over them, I accuse them of stopping me. The words come easily to mind and mouth. 'If it were not for so-and-so or such-and-such, I would be able to...' Instead of alleviating my lot, these complaints take me away from any real possibility of changing anything. I would simply be delegating my capacity to change to persons or objects over whom or which I obviously have no control. In other words, only if the scapegoat changes would I change.

Life can also present me with so many choices and interests that I have to skim from one to the other while the depth of the real pleasure of living escapes me. I alternate between fascination and boredom, total involvement and dejection, because I do not address the deeper questions. Is this or that activity really beneficial for me and those with whom I have contact? Will this or that interest truly lead me to a state of contentment? Again the years pass by and I look back on what could or should have been done and wasn't. Remorse becomes the only return of wasted time, money, energy or talent.

If I am fortunate, life becomes a great school. Behind apparent difficulties are my major lessons. Disguised in fleeting interests and routine tasks are the signposts that point me back towards truth. Relationships that bring with them repeated scenes of pettiness or bitterness with the same person and for the same reasons serve to show me the weaknesses I have to work on. Indeed, until I work on their transformation, I condemn myself to repeating them.

Challenges confront me, just to bring out the best in me. If I have the eyes to see and the courage to go forward, life is a constant experience of reminders and incentives to move progressively along the pathway to my highest consciousness.

IMPROVING THE QUALITY OF LIFE

The urge to improve takes birth in my innate sense of what is true and good. It would be difficult to find anyone who, given the chance, would refuse to better him or herself. The problem is, that we are experts in putting change off until a later date: 'tomorrow', 'next weekend', 'during the holidays', 'when I retire' become the catchwords of my lack of motivation.

As was seen in the fourth chapter, I am responsible for my life and acts. No one else thinks my thoughts or speaks my words for me. Whatever I sow, I reap in all three ways: thoughts, words and actions. Perhaps it's the daunting nature of this responsibility that turns me into an inveterate procrastinator.

A simple analysis of my life shows that the time required to get through the basics of living leaves very little over for other things. Obviously, if I want to improve the quality of my life, it has to include the basics. An improved life means better quality sleep, more satisfactory work and family life, better eating habits and use of free time – even better use of the time that I have to spend in apparently useless activities, such as traffic jams and queues!

If I look back over the first four chapters, I will find the inspiration necessary to marry ideals and practice.

THE JOURNEY SO FAR

Without a doubt the starting point of my journey is to know myself as a spiritual entity called *soul* expressing myself through the physical body,

The sense of self-identity gives me a solid grounding in life dynamics. Instead of a disorganised mental swirl of roles, responsibilities, relationships and routines, I discover the central point from which I can administer my life. The web we weave with our thoughts becomes untangled and the clarity to do whatever is best is strengthened.

By understanding the inner workings of the self, I can start to clear my mind, strengthen my intellect and elevate my *sanskars*. They become my first co-operators in empowering and improving the quality of my life. I discover my most basic *sanskars* of love, peace, purity, happiness, power, balance and truth and begin to access them in a very special way. Each small advance on the path, every tiny victory fills me with just a little more confidence of being able to arrive at my zenith. Things that used to trouble me become the silent witnesses of my progress, as I move with greater calm through tests relating to them. Situations that used to block my way start to open up to let me pass. I understand that my vision of the world was greatly conditioned by my own fears and desires. I see myself in the same world with the same people and tasks but I am somehow different.

Knowing others as spiritual beings similar to myself I can look at them with greater tolerance and openness. Prejudice, based on body type, sex, colour or age, no longer clouds my appreciation of humanity.

The initial steps in meditation help me to filter the information that comes in from my different life situations so that its effect on me is positive. The situation may be apparently difficult but the new self-confidence gained from meditation practice gives me the added courage to transform problems into challenges and solutions. By taking time out to remember what I truly am, I can continually reposition myself according to what's going on around me. If the external situation requires patience, I have greater ease in mustering it. If the need is determined action, I can summon it. I remember that whatever I do or become depends on my own ability to garner my own inner resources and use them appropriately.

Self-improvement brings me a sense of purpose. If, with all my failings, I can improve, then humanity has hope! By gradually throwing off my self-imposed limitations I understand how great my pact with mediocrity was. The unspoken conspiracy to remain within the norms of error and weakness ceases to have the hold on me that it once did. By working on improving my attitude towards the things that are within my reach — my home, family, work and so on — my life opens up to higher possibilities.

THE GOD FACTOR

If the strength to take the first steps on my journey upward depends on developing the consciousness of my true spiritual identity, it obviously includes the awareness of the context of where I am, where I come from and where I am going. The inner pilgrimage has really only one aim — the meeting and experience with God, the Supreme Mother-Father who has been my unconscious destination throughout the history of my births.

The most stable mind, the most far-reaching of intellects and the ocean of unlimited love, peace, happiness, truth, purity and balance that God is, has, to some extent, always been the beacon to guide me home. Lesser minds, intellects and personalities have appeared along the way but there has always been something that told me that I hadn't arrived, that, no matter how great the human being, I could really only be fulfilled by the source of all goodness. By linking my thoughts with that One I get the power to implement positive changes in all the aspects of my life.

Through closeness with God as the essence of all relationships — Mother, Father, Teacher, Guide, Friend and so on, my emotional needs are satisfied. Familiarity with that One helps me to overcome my own unfounded superstitions about what God does and does not do. I am no longer the beggar, pleading at the door of the Supreme One, but I recognise my rights.

If I used to express my need as 'Oh God, please forgive me', I now find I have first to forgive myself. If I used to plead 'Oh God, have mercy on me', I now work to have mercy on myself. Best of all, if I used to say, 'Oh God, please free me from my bondages', I perceive His divine amusement when He tells me: 'Child, let go of them. They are not binding you. It is you who are holding them to yourself'. In short, I take up the responsibility for what I create in my life, conquering the feeling of impotence that was given me by the idea that all life is random or an act of God's will.

With the help of the God factor I can get to my journey's end.

Other Eternity Ink meditation books and CDs are available.
For a catalogue contact:
Eternity Ink, First Floor, 77 Allen Street, Leichhardt NSW Australia 2040
Email: bkmedia@ozemail.com.au   www.bkmedia.com.au
www.brahmakumaris.com.au

Eternity Ink is the publisher for the Brahma Kumaris World Spiritual University.
If you wish to find out about the free meditation courses offered by the
Brahma Kumaris World Spiritual University, contact the main centre closest to you:

UK:	International Co-ordinating Office
	65 Pound Lane, London, NW10 2HH, UK www.bkwsu.com
	Tel (20) 8727 3350 Email: london@bkwsu.com
AUSTRALIA:	78 Alt Street, Ashfield, Sydney NSW 2131
	Tel (2) 9716 7066 Email: ashfield@au.bkwsu.org
BRAZIL:	R. Dona Germaine Burchard, 589 – Sao Paulo, SP 05002-062
	Tel (11) 3864 3694 Email: saopaulo@bkumaris.org.br
CHINA:	17 Dragon Road, Causeway Bay, Hong Kong
	Tel (852) 2806 3008 Email: rajainfo@rajayoga.com.hk
INDIA:	25 New Rohtak Road, Karol Bagh, New Delhi, 110005
	Tel (11) 2355 0355 Email: bkpbd@vsnl.com
KENYA:	Global Museum
	Maua Close, off Parklands Road, Westlands, Nairobi
	Tel (2) 3743 572 Email: bkwsugm@holidaybazaar.com
RUSSIA:	2 Gospitalnaya Ploschad, Building 1, Moscow 111020
	Tel (95) 263 02 47 Email: bkwsu@mail.ru
USA:	Global Harmony House
	46 Sth Middle Neck Rd, Great Neck NY 11021
	Tel (516) 773 0971 Email: newyork@bkwsu.com

You may be interested in using the Pathways Workbook *to help you go deeper into the* Pathways *ideas.*

PATHWAYS TO HIGHER CONSCIOUSNESS WORKBOOK

by Ken O'Donnell
Need training in soul-consciousness? Companion workbook to Pathways to Higher Consciousness, it gives easy, thought-provoking exercises for stepping along the pathway of a spiritual life. With ample room for writing and drawing. Enjoy exploring!
ISBN 0 9587230 5 2   CODE #230

Other titles exploring Raja Yoga Mediation teaching and philosophy for beginners:

BOOKS

PRACTICAL MEDITATION

An ideal textbook for the Raja Yoga Introductory Course. Each chapter takes a basic aspect of Raja Yoga knowledge and explains these deep concepts in simple language. Chapters finish with a short meditation to help you get started in the right direction.
ISBN 09592271 1 3   CODE #203

WISDOM THROUGH SPIRITUALITY

by Anthony Strano
The journey taken to discover spirituality is the most important journey the human soul can make. It is a journey within. Wisdom Through Spirituality is about that journey and how taking it enables us to become more than we ever thought possible.
ISBN 0 73440150 7   CODE #229

AUDIO CDs

TEACH YOURSELF TO MEDITATE

Presentations and commentaries by Sister Jayanti
Dive deep into the essence of Raja Yoga with two concepts – the soul, the point of energy and the Supreme Soul, whose spiritual qualities empower your transformation.
CODE #555

KNOWING MYSELF

Presentations and commentaries by Sister Jayanti
Learning to take your attention in a natural inward direction, to harness your own peace, love and joy. Effortlessly focus on the reality of the self.
CODE #745

KNOWING GOD

Presentations and commentaries by Sister Jayanti
As I travel beyond the physical dimension into a world of silence and stillness, I can experience God as a being of Light and Truth. Gently exploring the awareness of the Supreme Being as the Parent, Teacher and Friend.
CODE #746